"Someone once said that faith is not a personal possession until you have suffered. Faith requires the grit and courage to pray in the dark, the determination to become someone who can see it, lead in, and lean into the dark."
Nancy Ortberg, CEO of Transforming the Bay with Christ

"In so many ways prayer is ground zero for our faith, the ⸻ we hope, fear, and believe are intertwined deep within our ⸻ Liz Ditty gets it. She guides the reader into this sacred spac⸻ ness. Friend, whatever your current relationship to prayer, ⸻ whole self to this Bible study and find God's presence here."
Catherine McNiel, author of *Fearing Bravely: Risking Love for Our Neighbors, Strangers, and Enemies*

"With her distinct mix of depth, warmth, and pastoral sensitivity, Liz Ditty once again helps us draw closer to the God who so longs for nearness with us. This journey through Elijah's story and the Lord's Prayer will inspire and equip you to experience God more deeply through the ups, downs, and in-betweens of life."
Jay Y. Kim, pastor and author of *Analog Christian*

"If we are honest, we all long for deeper communion with God and yet find ourselves often stuck or frustrated in our time of prayer. In *Hear My Prayer*, my friend Liz honestly shares our struggle in prayer and offers a path forward integrating biblical insights, spiritual practices, and practical wisdom into a meaningful and life-giving praying life. Whether you are a new or seasoned follower of Jesus, this book will stir greater hope and intimacy with God!"
David Kim, discipleship and formation pastor at WestGate Church and author of *Made to Belong*

"What a fresh perspective on prayer you hold in your hands! With creativity and keen biblical insight, Liz Ditty shows us how to attune to God in a fresh way. If you feel lost in how to pray or dry in your experience of God's presence, this study is a tall glass of water for your soul. Our culture is thirsty to experience God in uncertainty, through the hard work of forgiveness, and in the darkness of the valley. Liz Ditty gently takes our hand, gives us excellent practices to try, and walks with us there."
Amy Seiffert, Bible teacher and author of *Starved*

"This unique Bible study invites readers to not only meditate on biblical passages but also apply it to their lives in contemplative, creative ways both individually and in community. It goes beyond a traditional question-and-answer model and engages almost all your senses, as you learn the foundations of a vibrant prayer life by examining Elijah's story and Jesus' prayer. Whether you want to recharge your prayer life or learn how to pray, Liz Ditty's gentle writing style and solid biblical teaching will encourage you to make conversations with God integral to your life and will deepen your intimacy with God."
Mabel Ninan, author of *Far from Home: Discovering Your Identity as Foreigners on Earth*

HEAR MY PRAYER

LEARNING

FROM THE

FAITH OF

ELIJAH

LIZ DITTY

A **6-WEEK** BIBLE
STUDY EXPERIENCE

IVP
Bible
Studies

An imprint of InterVarsity Press
Downers Grove, Illinois

InterVarsity Press
P.O. Box 1400 | Downers Grove, IL 60515-1426
ivpress.com | email@ivpress.com

InterVarsity Press® is the publishing division of InterVarsity Christian Fellowship/USA®. For more information, visit intervarsity.org.

All Scripture quotations, unless otherwise indicated, are taken from The Holy Bible, New International Version®, NIV®. Copyright © 1973, 1978, 1984, 2011 by Biblica, Inc.™ Used by permission of Zondervan. All rights reserved worldwide. www.zondervan.com. The "NIV" and "New International Version" are trademarks registered in the United States Patent and Trademark Office by Biblica, Inc.™

Published in association with the literary agent Don Gates of The Gates Group, www.the-gates-group.com.

While any stories in this book are true, some names and identifying information may have been changed to protect the privacy of individuals.

Interior art by Janine Crum, www.janinecrum.com. Used by permission.

"Ever Enough" by Bre Erb. Used with permission.

"Patient Trust" by Pierre Teilhard de Chardin, translated by Michael Harter. © The Institute of Jesuit Sources at Boston College, Chestnut Hill, MA. Used by permission.

The publisher cannot verify the accuracy or functionality of website URLs used in this book beyond the date of publication.

Cover design: David Fassett
Interior design: Jeanna Wiggins
Cover images: Getty Images: © fotograzia / Moment, © Iakov Zaiats / iStock, © Akintevs / iStock, © Pobytov / DigitalVision Vectors

ISBN 978-1-5140-0623-8 (print) | ISBN 978-1-5140-0624-5 (digital)

Printed in the United States of America ♾

Library of Congress Cataloging-in-Publication Data
A catalog record for this book is available from the Library of Congress.

30 29 28 27 26 25 24 | 8 7 6 5 4 3 2 1

CONTENTS

INTRODUCTION

AS A LITTLE GIRL, I would stand in socked feet on top of my dad's shoes while he tried to teach me how to dance on the yellowed kitchen linoleum. "When it's your wedding, you dance with your dad first," he said sternly. "Only when I let the groom cut in can he take you out of my arms."

He couldn't know then that he was the one who would be taken from my arms, not the other way around. While people earnestly prayed outside his hospital room for a miracle, I did not. Stage-four brain cancer was something I prayed to accept, not for God to heal.

My wedding was only four months away, and the doctors believed he had six to twelve months to live. He might be in a wheelchair, but his goofy grin could still light up the dance floor. *I'm not even asking to keep him, Lord, just one last dance in the window you've already given him to live.* For all the deals humans have made with God, I was shooting for an easy yes.

When my dad took his last breath, I glanced down at my left hand resting near his knee. My engagement ring shimmered against the rough hospital blanket. It was ten weeks before my wedding day.

No one told me about the scars that calcify around unanswered prayers, or how to grapple with disappointment in God that wheels uncontrollably toward anger. I was distracted enough navigating the countless losses that rippled outward from losing my dad, and at the same time propelled forward by the excitement of starting a brand-new life with my husband. And life kept going.

I didn't stop believing in God, I couldn't lose him too. We had been through too much together and I was sure he had his reasons. I kept reading my Bible, continued to lead in our church, and I still prayed. But my prayers became . . . *small.*

Life without expectation isn't life without disappointment; it's life without hope.

My imagination of God had slowly shifted to someone I could trust for his vast knowledge and wisdom, but whose plan couldn't be changed by my prayers. A God who refused to answer the smallest, purest request from his loyal servant, for a reason too vast for me to know. When I was young, after I got shots at the doctor, I always got to drive through McDonald's and get an ice cream cone to take a little bit of the sting away. I figured God just wasn't that kind of Father.

I know my unanswered prayer is smaller than some of yours. Not trusting God to know and do good is the oldest mistake in the Bible. It's the fundamental lie that Satan told humans in the Garden of Eden, and it took me over a decade of unspoken prayers to realize I had begun believing it. My image of God had shifted toward wise and powerful, away from caring and kind.

Have you ever considered how your prayers (answered or not) have shaped your idea of what God is like? The way we talk to God—or don't—can reveal something hidden that we believe about who God is. *An inescapable part of prayer is getting comfortable in the presence of God.* For the next six weeks, we will move toward less awkward, more authentic conversations with God. We'll experiment with different ways to talk to God and practice holding—not hiding—our resistance to prayer that has settled in.

This Bible study will immerse us in the story of the prophet Elijah. You may have heard people talk about Elijah hearing God whisper to him in 1 Kings 19. James, the brother of Jesus, tells the story with a twist—Elijah didn't just listen to God, God listened to Elijah. When Elijah prayed, fire burst down from heaven, food appeared for the starving, and rain refused to fall. James doesn't put this forward as a mythic example or something only great prophets achieve; in James 5:17 he writes, "Elijah was a human being, even as we are. He prayed earnestly that it would not rain, and it did not rain on the land for three and a half years."

I couldn't imagine praying for rain or fire or resurrection like Elijah, even if he was human. When Jesus' disciples wondered how to pray, he taught them with his prayer.

This, then, is how you should pray:

"Our Father in heaven,
 hallowed be your name,
 your kingdom come,
 your will be done,
     on earth as it is in heaven.
 Give us today our daily bread.
 And forgive us our debts,
     as we also have forgiven our debtors.
 And lead us not into temptation,
     but deliver us from the evil one." (Matthew 6:9-13)

It turns out the things Jesus taught his followers to pray for were just the kind of things that Elijah prayed for, that James reminded the early church they could pray for, and that humans like us have prayed for ever since. Let's spend some time in Jesus' prayer with the human Elijah and see if we can find the same courage, wonder, and new life that he found in his conversations with God.

In Sunday school I was taught that God answered every prayer with one of three answers: yes, no, or wait. God always seemed to answer mine with silence, which was supposed to be a no or wait, and that never felt like much of an answer at all. I now know that God answers my prayers in an infinite number of ways. Sometimes he answers a prayer about my job with a word from someone else about my identity. Sometimes when I pray for my kids' health, he answers with his own calming presence. There are more than three answers. They don't fit on a traffic light. *God has as many words and ways to meet us as a living, breathing, eternally wise, and boundlessly loving Father.* I wonder what prayers we will bring to God in the coming weeks, or if those prayers will change, or how they will change us. All I can promise is that God is listening.

HOW TO USE
THIS BOOK

WHETHER YOU ARE ENGAGING in this study with a large group, a small group, a friend, or on your own, here are some helpful suggestions.

FOR THE GROUP SESSION . . .

Set aside a designated day and time for a weekly gathering—in person or virtually—for the next six weeks. The content (video, discussion, and prayer) will take about ninety minutes.

The videos are accessed through the QR code in the book. These videos were created with a group in mind, so you can watch the video together and immediately engage in the content that follows. Everyone with a book can access the videos, so if you miss a group session it is easy to stay in the loop. If you're studying on your own, you can still watch the videos, and each group session includes adaptations just for you.

A few tips on engaging in the group sessions:

1. As your group comes together, it is an opportunity to create a space where all people and stories are welcome. Creating a place to be seen and belong connects us with one another. Together we can encourage each other as we move toward more honest and intimate prayers.

2. Pray every day, even if it's only for a minute. Pray for whatever is on your heart and for your group—for individual prayer requests or for the group to experience God meaningfully.

3. Embrace curiosity as a core value. If someone's thoughts about God or personal stories surprise you, remember that God is not surprised. Listen to understand them better and leave space for them to change their mind (or yours!) over the course of your time together.

4. This study includes a variety of art, music, poetry, and other creative elements to point you toward the presence of God—as well as invitations to create your own art. If you don't consider yourself an artist, lean in and try something new!

5. Remember that anything said in the group is considered confidential and should not be discussed outside the group unless specific permission is given.

This study is designed so that you can still participate in the group session that launches each new week even if you haven't done all the homework, but I hope you'll still *want* to engage with everything!

FOR THE INDIVIDUAL DAYS . . .

Following the group session are five days of content for you to engage with during the week between group gatherings. The content is meaningful but not overwhelming, and it's designed to be a gift to your busy life. Each week includes:

- **Three days of study**. Plan to invest fifteen to twenty minutes in reading each day. You'll also find space for reflection as a gift for you on every day of study. It's an opportunity to care for yourself and might extend your time to thirty minutes.

- **One day of prayer**. Every week has a prayer day to focus on a particular type or method of prayer. Some of these may be familiar to you, and some may be an invitation to try new ways of talking to God.

- **One day of following a practice**. Enjoy a restorative day at the end of each week with helpful tools to engage with God and with your own story.

A few tips for engaging in individual study and reflection:

1. Start with prayer. As you begin each day, invite God to speak to you through his Word.

2. Keep your Bible handy. You'll be using it to look up passages.

3. If you don't have time to fully dive in to any of the reflections, prayers, or practices during the week, schedule time for yourself to catch up on any you missed. You can look forward to some intentional soul care.

4. Share your ideas. As you reflect, journal, and talk to God, share what you are thinking about with people you care about, not just those in your study group.

HONEST PRAYERS

Our Father, who art in heaven,
hallowed be thy name.

We must know before we can love. In order to know God,
we must often think of Him; and when we come to love Him,
we shall then also think of Him often, for our
heart will be with our treasure.

BROTHER LAWRENCE

GROUP SESSION

We can be told God is all-powerful, all-knowing, or always present—but none of that matters if we don't know that he's also good.

GETTING STARTED

Prayer is a conversation, and our conversations vary wildly depending on who we're talking to and our relationship with them.

We're not only going to spend the next six weeks studying prayer—but we're also going to pray! Turn to the back of this book to the Daily Prayer Commitment Tracker, and we'll start our work for Day 4 early. What prayer goal could you set for yourself every day this week, even if it is something small?

VIEW THE WEEK ONE VIDEO

Notes

- Elijah was a complex human.

- Elijah's story is more than a highlight reel.

- Elijah's prayers were honest.

DISCUSS

1. What are your clearest memories that have shaped your understanding of what God is like?

2. Take a look at this list of ways the Bible describes God:

Compassionate	Kind	Patient	Loyal
Forgiver	Judge of evil	Healer	Provider
Wisdom	Comfort	Worthy	Creator
Powerful	Victory	Protector	Peace
Vindicator	Freedom	Second chances	Joyful

3. Which attributes do you know to be true about God? Circle the ones that resonate with you most, or make a note if there is an important one that is missing from this partial list.

4. Is there a reason or an experience that made those attributes stand out to you?

5. Are there any truths about who God is that you wish were more evident in your own experience of him? How can the people surrounding you help you pray with hope for God to be visible in those ways right now?

ALL TOGETHER: GOD IS LIKE . . .

Materials needed: Leaders can head to www.lizditty.com/prayer to print out the metaphor tiles, then lay them face up in a place that is easy for everyone to see.

What is God like? Our attitude toward prayer is determined by our understanding of who God is. What would he be like if he were in the same room as you? What would he say or do? Would he sit or stand? Roll his eyes? Laugh? Scowl? We all have life experiences, or family traditions, or stories we have picked up from somewhere that shape our idea of what God is like.

Words can only describe so much. Choose a photo tile from the previous page that represents something about your impression of God.

1. What aspect of God's character or your relationship with him does this image capture?

2. Were there any images that did not resonate at all?

3. How could knowing and remembering who God is change the way you talk to him?

4. If you are comfortable, share your responses.

PRAYING TOGETHER: TO THE RIGHT *(15 minutes)*

Closing the group time, take the opportunity to share where in your life you would like to see God move in all his glory and goodness. Listen closely to the person sitting on your right. After everyone has shared, go around the circle again and pray for the person to your right.

SOLO STUDY

Some easy adjustments if you are on this journey with us, but without a group:

- Choose your photo tile(s) and journal your answers to the prompts.
- Share one of your favorite memories of connecting with God—with a person you know or on social media.
- The next time someone mentions something worrying them, ask if you can pray for them.

DAY 1 — Read Luke 18:9-14

Our posture when we pray has to do with our image of God and also our image of ourselves. In his Gospel, Luke loves to tell the stories of reversals. This parable is no exception. While I'm not sure either character is fully relatable for me (they are extreme opposites), the story still feels familiar. Jesus warns us about one posture in prayer while praising another, so we'll look at both as well as other prayer postures that are common today.

OVERLY CONFIDENT POSTURE

Your anxiety about praying in public may ramp up as you realize you have begun a group study on prayer. When you look at this Pharisee, you should begin to feel better. The Pharisees were the religious elite of Jesus' day. They had intense theological training and a mountain of knowledge about laws and culture. They knew lots of Scripture by heart and were the spiritual luminaries in every room they entered. Sometimes, if we're new to praying in groups or tend to be more introverted, we might think we're missing something important or don't know how to pray. This man had everything we think we're supposed to have, and Jesus said his prayer was pretty terrible. Why?

When we read it, it's easy to see pride, entitlement, and looking down on others. Our prayers aren't a performance to make us look good or sound good to anyone who can hear. Jesus told this parable to people who loved the sound of their own voice as a big warning that our attitude will ruin our prayers much faster than our words.

HUMBLE POSTURE

The second man had a simple prayer, acknowledging his need for mercy. When we hear of someone beating their chest, it sounds a bit dramatic and attention drawing; don't worry, that is not our activity today! In that social context, this man was publicly expressing his repentance. In this great reversal, Jesus contrasted the most respected person in society—the Pharisee—with the least respected, most hated person. Tax collectors were stereotypically sellouts to Israel's political oppressors, who ignored the laws the Pharisees kept and were considered greedy thieves. God doesn't see what we see, though. He sees the posture and the heart of the prayer, not the person's words or reputation.

The postures of prayer that most tempt me to close off from God are slightly different from these. I wonder if they feel familiar to you, or if you have others you would add.

TENTATIVE POSTURE

One of the biggest hurdles to prayer is simply being unsure of what to say or how to say it. I know many people who struggle with knowing how formal to be or with not wanting to talk casually to God. Does prayer have to be a set-aside time with intentionality, or does it count to whisper your need for a parking space? When you approach God are you nervous that you aren't allowed to be there? It can be helpful to build familiarity over time; you don't have to talk to God as if he's your best friend if he isn't. Hopefully at the end of this week, you can begin to be more comfortable with not only the greatness but also the goodness and patience of God.

SKEPTICAL POSTURE

Does prayer actually change anything? One of the most common enemies of prayer is believing we don't need it or prayer doesn't change anything. Søren Kierkegaard observed, "The function of Prayer is not to influence God, but rather to change the nature of the one who prays." I will confess that prayer has not solved all the problems in my life, or even helped me understand them. Still it has helped me walk through seemingly impossible things and connected me to others while doing that. It's true, what James 5:17 says—our prayers can be as powerful as those of Elijah or Jesus—but it's no guarantee that our prayers will always have the effect we want. If there is one thing that keeps me praying with hope in a world that can feel chaotic and unfair, it's prayer itself. There is no refuge from the unbearable like the presence of God; there's nowhere else I would rather be when I'm confused or stuck. Skepticism is lonely and unavailable for the surprise of answered prayer or maybe even a miracle; it doesn't protect us—it imprisons us.

We are all invited to pray with an open posture—not always perfect prayers or powerful prayers, but open, honest prayers, knowing who we are and who God is in the right proportions and letting our conversations with him change us as much as they change our circumstances.

REFLECTION: WELCOMING PRAYER

A humble posture in prayer doesn't always look like beating our chests, declaring what a big sinner we are. It can simply mean that we surrender to the wisdom and goodness of God instead of forcing our way. We walk through the hallway of our interior soul and remove the Do Not Enter signs we have posted on certain doors. There are parts of our thoughts or lives that we struggle to have God enter because we don't want him to change things or mess them up or tell us to do something we don't want to hear. These welcoming prayers will help us pray in an open posture. They have been adapted from Adele Ahlberg Calhoun's *Spiritual Disciplines Handbook*.

Take a deep breath and choose three of these welcoming prayers to pray or make your own. Choose the areas you most need the goodness and greatness of God to be part of.

- Jesus, I let go of my need to control my relationships. Welcome.
- Jesus, I let go of my need to control my career. Welcome.
- Jesus, I let go of my need to control my circumstances. Welcome.
- Jesus, I let go of my need to control newspaper headlines. Welcome.
- Jesus, I let go of my need to control my mental health without help. Welcome.
- Jesus, I let go of my need to control what other people think about me. Welcome.

- Jesus, I let go of my need to control my level of impact on the world. Welcome.

- Jesus, I let go of my need to control _____. Welcome.

DAY 2

In the Gospels, Jesus often goes off by himself to pray apart from his closest friends. The relationship Jesus had with his Father was eternal and incredibly close; Jesus said "I and the Father are one" (John 10:30). But when Jesus took on a human body and the full human experience that goes with it, he talked to God by praying.

His disciples were curious about how to talk to God, so Jesus told them,

This, then, is how you should pray:

"Our Father in heaven,
hallowed be your name,
your kingdom come,
your will be done,
    on earth as it is in heaven.
Give us today our daily bread.
And forgive us our debts,
    as we also have forgiven our debtors.
And lead us not into temptation,
    but deliver us from the evil one." (Matthew 6:9-13)

You might recognize these verses as the Lord's Prayer, the outline for our six weeks together. They are the prayers Jesus teaches us to pray—and the kinds of prayers that Elijah prayed. We'll explore these themes more in the coming weeks, but let's notice that Jesus prayed like a human too. I wonder if it was strange for him, having always communicated one way with God, to pray to God instead. It makes me think of the first time my husband and I were apart for a week while we were still dating, and of just looking at him and knowing what he was thinking, I had to text him. I imagine Jesus aching to be with God, but he learned how to pray—and taught us.

Jesus knew God better than anyone else, and he wanted to make God known to us. Beyond his most famous prayer, Jesus told us a lot about what God is like and what prayer is like.

Jesus also taught his disciples what God is like. For each of the passages below, draw a line to connect each passage with the summary of what Jesus is saying about his Father.

WHAT JESUS TEACHES US TO EXPECT FROM GOD IN PRAYER

Matthew 6:8 and Matthew 6:32	God honors persistent prayers.
Matthew 6:26 and Matthew 10:29	When we feel unseen, God sees us.
Luke 18:1-7	God cares about us.
Luke 18:11-13	God knows what we need.
Matthew 6:6	God gives good gifts.

How does Jesus' list of what God is like compare to the list from the group session or the image you chose for yourself? List anything about God you appreciated being reminded about this week:

REFLECTION: WHO'S WHO

When we pray to God, we're praying to the entire Trinity of God the Father, the Son, and the Holy Spirit. Each member of the Trinity plays an important part in our prayers.

What does God do as we pray? (Luke 11:9-13; 1 John 5:14-15)

What does Jesus do as we pray? (Hebrews 4:14-16)

What does the Holy Spirit do as we pray? (Matthew 10:19-21; Romans 8:26-27)

What are you doing when you pray? (Ephesians 6:17-18; Philippians 4:6-7)

Do you feel like you need help to pray the kinds of prayers you want to pray, or to pray as much as you hope to, or to even pray at all? What kind of help could you ask for from the Father, Jesus, the Holy Spirit, or other humans who pray?

Many people don't give themselves enough credit for their prayer life. Saint Augustine wrote, "True, whole prayer is nothing but love." Do you find your mind drifting into a conversation with God as you fall asleep? Noticing his beauty and goodness in your life and giving him credit? Appreciating him as you listen to or sing certain kinds of music? All of that counts as love and prayer. Think of how the Holy Spirit might translate that in heaven.

Jesus' prayer has been a model for me since childhood. I can't even recite "Our Father, who art in heaven . . ." without rolling out the words in a liturgical cadence. Those four concise verses have inspired countless meditations and writings, including mine. Not too long ago, though, my prayers felt like they were being whispered into a wilderness. It wasn't until I saw God respond to Elijah's prayers that my own prayers made sense to me.

In Elijah's story, I recognized my own fears, insecurities, expectations, and confusion. I can't wait for you to meet the God Elijah knew, the one we'll know better for having seen him through the prophet's eyes. Elijah's most famous prayer called down fire from heaven, but he prayed so many prayers before and after that—for justice, for the healing of others, and even one for giving up. Long before Jesus taught his disciples how to pray, Elijah intuitively prayed the kinds of prayers that Jesus said were possible. Elijah even had the audacity to ask God for things that no one else imagined were possible. We have so much to learn from him about trusting God to be closer than we realize—and just as much about relying on God when he appears absent. Jesus' brother James reminds us that Elijah was a *human just like us*: "Elijah was a human being, even as we are. He prayed earnestly that it would not rain, and it did not rain on the land for three and a half years" (James 5:17).

Elijah's prayers were powerful because of the God he prayed them to. He had a lot of faith, but that's because Elijah knew the Father.

> Elijah's prayers were powerful because of the God he prayed them to. He had a lot of faith, but that's because Elijah knew the Father.

"Our Father, who art in heaven, hallowed be thy name." Who taught Elijah what God was like? How did he know what kind of father he was praying to or what sort of things he could ask for?

There are a lot of things we don't know, but as a faithful Israelite, we can be relatively certain that Elijah was very familiar with the story of Moses. There are many, many parallels between the life of Elijah and the life of Moses. I've included a few; take time to fill in the blanks.

PARALLELS BETWEEN THE LIVES OF MOSES AND ELIJAH

	MOSES	ELIJAH
ANGEL APPEARS	Exodus 3:2	1 Kings 19:5
DEBATE WITH GOD	Exodus 3:7–4:17	1 Kings 19:9-18
GOD GIVES AN ASSISTANT	Exodus 24:13	1 Kings 19:16
PRAYERS CONTROLLED FIRE	Number 11:2	1 Kings 18:38
	Exodus 16:4	1 Kings 17:6
	Exodus 19:18-19	1 Kings 19:9-13
	Numbers 11:14-15	1 Kings 19:4
	Exodus 24:18	1 Kings 19:8

This is not even a complete list! Elijah seems to take notes from Moses on performing signs and plagues to display God's power to the royalty of their times, and Elijah was very aware of Moses' warnings to God's people who chose lesser gods.

As a faithful follower of God, Elijah would have been quite familiar with God's words to Moses recorded in Exodus 34. This meaningful introduction God makes for himself is repeated throughout Scripture. (See also 2 Chronicles 30:9; Nehemiah 9:17; Psalms 86:15; 103:8; 111:4; 145:8; Joel 2:13; Jonah 4:2.)

Take a pen or pencil and underline or circle all the characteristics of God.

> Then the LORD came down in the cloud and stood there with him and proclaimed his name, the LORD. And he passed in front of Moses, proclaiming, "The LORD, the LORD, the compassionate and gracious God, slow to anger, abounding in love and faithfulness, maintaining love to thousands, and forgiving wickedness, rebellion and sin. Yet he does not leave the guilty unpunished; he punishes the children and their children for the sin of the parents to the third and fourth generation." (Exodus 34:5-7)

As you look over those words and phrases that describe God, consider how these truths might change the way you think about God or the kinds of prayers you pray.

If God is compassionate and gracious, then I can talk to God about . . .

If God is slow to anger, then I can talk to God about . . .

If God is abounding in love and faithfulness, then I can talk to God about . . .

If God is about forgiving wickedness, rebellion, and sin, then I can tell God about . . .

If God does not leave the guilty unpunished, then I can talk to God about . . .

Elijah expected God to be faithful to him, to show divine compassion to vulnerable people he knew, and to punish the evil in his world with a God-sized justice so that he didn't have to be anxious or vengeful himself. I'm not sure I always remember who God is when I pray to him. Do you?

REFLECTION: A SPOKEN WORD

This spoken word was written by Bre Erb in reflection on Elijah's relationship with God. When we begin to understand who God is, it changes the way we feel about being near him. Read it here or watch her performance on www.lizditty.com/prayer.

EVER ENOUGH

God I've witnessed
First hand Your power
Like fire burning through
   the sky,
I watched as each flame
   swallowed the
   shackles of sin,
Yet not one of my hairs
   were singed.
No longer bound by flesh,
My knees buckled in
   surrender,
They met the pavement
   in an instant,
A cry of allegiance to You.

Miracle after miracle,
There's not enough ink in
   the world to document
Your faithfulness,
Not just in my life
But in all of those who
   bear Your image.
From the beginning of
   creation
To this very second,
Not for one moment,
Have You left us forsaken.
Whether from brooks
Or by the mouths of ravens,
Your provision never ceases
Yet I fail to see this

As I wander through desert
   seasons.

Countless prayers have
   slipped past my lips
Through clenched teeth
   and doubt,
I wonder if my requests have
   reached Heaven,
Or if in transit they got lost
   among the stars.
As I wait,
I can't help but look back.
Comparing or re-creating
Your presence,
Desperate to witness a
   glimpse of Your glory
Instead of trusting you're
   there for me,
Hidden in the whispers of
   cool and quiet caves.
Lord, I crave marvelous things,
Supernatural fire and winds
Parted seas and rain from
   cloudless skies,
I
Am hardly satisfied with
   simple whispers . . .
Yet it's in those moments,
I feel closest to You.

Will this ever be enough?

PRAYER: PRAYERS OF INTENTION

Our posture toward God in prayer is affected by what we expect him to be like, but it is also influenced by what we want from God. Take some time to reflect on what you are hoping your conversations with God will become. We all feel guilty that we don't pray enough—but "pray more" isn't the answer. What kind of conversation do you want to develop with God?

SETTING OUR INTENTIONS

What are you hoping will happen during this study on prayer?

What are you afraid might happen during this study on prayer?

Our intentions are more than just thoughts, they're plans. As you look at the weeks ahead, decide how much time you want to spend in prayer every day. You could start with five, ten, or even one minute a day. Maybe your goals are less about the amount of time and more about the priority or content of your prayers. For example, "This week I will pray before I drink my coffee." Or, "This week I will pray for my friend every day." Your goals may or may not change each week. No matter how often you complete the daily studies, try to pray every day.

Plan when you will dedicate time for praying each day. Will you set an alarm to get up early? Will your last words before you fall asleep be a prayer? You can download wallpaper for your mobile phone at www.lizditty.com/prayer to help you remember. You might even decide not to unlock your phone in the morning until you've talked to God about your day.

If it's helpful or motivating to you, you can use the Daily Prayer Commitment Tracker at the end of the book to track your prayer goal. For any days you missed, know that grace was already covering you on that day.

SURRENDERING OUR INTENTIONS

As we set intentions, we need God's grace so we don't chase after goals in the wrong direction. Take a moment to surrender your agenda, desires, intentions, and fears to God.

This Prayer of Abandonment is one I return to when there is something in my life beyond my control—something I cannot even fix or manage by prayer. I remember that all God is asking from me is myself. That his will is wise and good and safe to surrender to. As you read this prayer, feel free to make it your own. Add your own art or music, or change the language to be your own words. Offer it back to God as your own prayer.

PRAYER OF ABANDONMENT

Charles de Foucauld

Father,
I abandon myself into your hands;
do with me what you will.
Whatever you may do, I thank you:
I am ready for all, I accept all.
Let only your will be done in me,
and in all your creatures—
I wish no more than this, O Lord.
Into your hands I commend my soul;
I offer it to you with all the love of
my heart,
for I love you, Lord, and so need to
give myself,
to surrender myself into your hands
without reserve,
and with boundless confidence,
for you are my Father.
Amen.

DAY 5

PRACTICE: PRAYER OF EXAMEN

The Prayer of Examen is a prayer of awareness. It is a daily practice of noticing God's movements and remembering your actions throughout a period, usually the past day or days.

This exercise is a bit like a sit-up—the exercise itself is great, but it's the daily practice over time that makes an enormous difference. This might be something you try just once today, or a practice you continue through this study, or possibly something you return to during a difficult season.

Begin by resting in the love of God. No matter how good or bad you feel about your day or yourself, you are deeply loved by God. He is actively showing you love even now.

Ask for attention. Begin by finding a place to sit—feet grounded to the floor, body relaxed but with good posture, eyes open or closed—and take a few deep breaths. Then ask God to help you see the day that has passed and trace the Holy Spirit's presence.

Begin with gratitude. Take a moment to consider the things of your day, large or small, that you are grateful for. A spark of joy at a stranger's smile, a glance at an old photo, a thoughtful message from a friend, the golden hour before sunset. What made you notice the good gifts of beauty, love, or joy in your world today? Don't make a list of things you think you should be grateful for, revisit the moment and rest in gratitude.

Practice noticing. Reflect on the details of your day, what happened, and how you experienced the day's events.

- How did you wake up? How did you feel about the day when you woke up?

- What emotions did you feel during the day? Choose some specific words from the feelings wheel at the end of this section. Were your feelings represented in a lot of different colors or in mostly one?

- Where did you give, receive, or desire love?

- When did you feel connected or disconnected?

- What was your high point? Low point?

- Was there a complex problem or emotion that you did not have time to deal with?

- Was there anything that could have been the movement of the Holy Spirit?

- How do you feel as you end the day? What is your hope for tomorrow? If it is helpful, use the feelings wheel to find specific names for your emotions.

Talk to God. What stands out from your reflection? Are you feeling stuck anywhere? Is there a potential or possibility that is exciting to you? Is there shame or fear that you don't know how to hold? Talk to God like a friend, a compassionate listener who knows you and loves you no matter what. Take the opportunity to free yourself with confession and rest in his love.

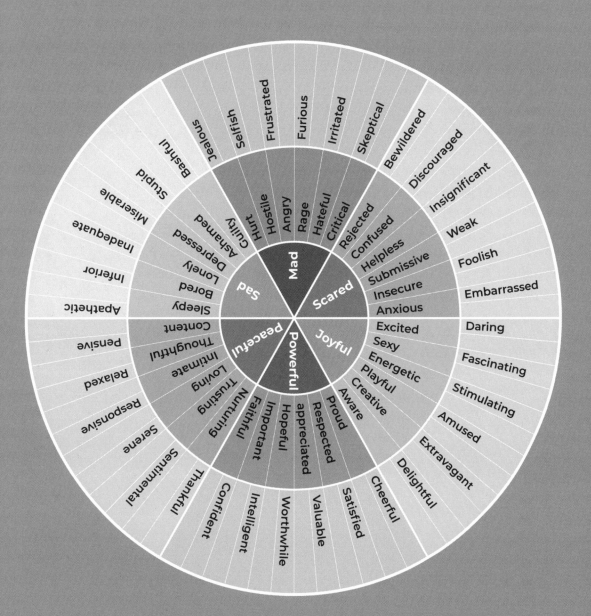

Feelings wheel

WEEK 2

UNEXPECTED ANSWERS

*Thy kingdom come, thy will be done,
on earth as it is in heaven.*

*So when Jesus directs us to pray, "Thy kingdom come,"
he does not mean we should pray for it to come into existence.
Rather, we pray for it to take over at all points in the personal,
social, and political order where it is now excluded: "On earth as
it is in heaven." With this prayer we are invoking it, as in faith
we are acting it, into the real world of our daily existence.*

DALLAS WILLARD

GROUP SESSION

Are we praying for God to change our world to be good according to his wisdom,
or for him to make things the way we want them to be?

SUMMARY OF WEEK ONE

- We considered our posture in prayer.
- Jesus told us what praying to our Father in heaven is like.
- We examined the way that God's people saw him in the Old Testament.

What stood out to you last week? Was there something from your study, your
life, or your conversations with God that you would like to share?

Notes

- God's answered prayer teaches us dependence on him, not independence from him.

- God's answered prayer teaches us expectation, not entitlement.

- The opportunity in our grief is to turn toward God, not away from him.

DISCUSS

1. What is your strategy when asking people for things you need? Is that ever hard for you?

2. Has God ever given you something you needed?

3. What do you think you need right now?

4. Is there something you are grieving right now? Can we pray with you as you heal?

ALL TOGETHER: REALLY BAD DRAWINGS

Materials Needed: A blank piece of paper and a writing tool for everyone. Colorful pencils, pens, or markers are optional.

No art skills are required! We're going to make some terrible drawings quickly. Stick figures and basic symbols are encouraged, but go for it if you want to show off. There are only three things that need to be in your drawing: (1) you, (2) your prayer, and (3) God.

- Imagine yourself praying. Quickly sketch yourself praying in whatever setting you think of.

- Now draw the things you are praying about as pictures, symbols, or words.

- Now write God's name or draw something that represents God as he is listening to your prayer.

Conversation

1. Can you tell us about your picture?

2. How do you experience yourself and God when you pray? How do the size, location, distances, or elements of your picture portray your attitudes about prayer or God (even if you did not intentionally draw them in a certain way)?

3. How would you like your prayers to be the same as we grow together?

4. How would you like your prayers to be different as we grow together?

PRAYING TOGETHER: A BIGGER PICTURE *(10 minutes)*

Materials needed: The same drawing tools and the picture you just drew.

Thank you for sharing your picture of you, your prayer, and God. Now add your group to the picture! Where would it be most helpful for them to be present? Can they support you? Share the weight of your prayer requests? Show up in the space between you and God as a bridge to him or representation of him? Let them know!

Depending on the size of your group, you might share with everyone or with a smaller group and then pray together, being mindful to enter one another's stories in the places where invited.

Some easy adjustments if you are on this journey with us, but without a group:

- Draw your own really bad drawing! What stands out to you?

- Is there anyone you can ask to pray with you about the things that matter most?

DAY 1   *Read 1 Kings 16:29–17:7*

Elijah appears out of nowhere. The first time his name drops on the page, he is standing before the mighty King Ahab, and Elijah is not lacking confidence. In the New International Version Elijah says, "God . . . whom I serve," but in the King James Version and others, Elijah says, "God . . . before whom I stand." Elijah stood in the presence of God. *What was that like?* We don't get the same inner view into Elijah's calling that we do with Isaiah (Isaiah 6) or Jeremiah (Jeremiah 1:4-10). Still, after his encounter with God, Elijah begins his prophetic ministry with passion and purpose.

Have you ever sensed that you were standing in God's presence? What was that like?

If you could stand before God, what do you wish he would say?

Elijah has a message God gave him: "There will be neither dew nor rain in the next few years except at my word."

This announcement of drought isn't wholly unexpected. King Ahab led God's people into worshiping Baal, a pagan god of Canaan who was one of the most significant gods worshiped throughout the Middle East in the ancient era.

For the king of God's people to institutionalize national worship of God's enemy was a deep betrayal. Ahab needed to recognize that he had rejected God, abused his authority, manipulated the people, and made *big* changes, not just personally but nationally. Sometimes God's most incredible mercy is his discipline. It can put us on the path to seeing how broken the mess we made is and ultimately move us toward making things right. Of course, we always have the option to stubbornly ignore God and his wisdom no matter how far he goes to get our attention. Sadly, that will be the way of Ahab.

While the Bible doesn't give us many details about Baal, we know from historical texts that he was a fertility god and called, among other things, "Lord of Rain and Dew" and "He Who Rides on Clouds."

So who's the God of rain? Well, we are about to find out. While some people look at the Old Testament and see false gods as empty and powerless, that's not how the Bible describes them. Yes, idols were nothing powerful on their own (Isaiah 44:9; 1 Corinthians 8:4), but false gods were not just figments of imagination. In Israel's history, Moses went to Pharaoh on behalf of God to demand the release of his people from the brutality of Egyptian slavery. God empowered Moses to prove his representation of God through miracles, signs, and plagues. Pharaoh's magicians were unimpressed with many of the signs because their gods could do those things too (Exodus 7:11-12, 22). So whose power did they represent? God has had enemies, spiritual beings, from the very beginning. While they can't compare to the power of God, they are still very powerful. We use the term Satan now to refer to the chief enemy of God, and we call his supporters demons. Baal may have been an impressive demon or perhaps the spirit we know as Satan.

Notice how God's enemy, Baal, tried to impersonate God. Baal called himself the god of life (fertility and rain) when it was God who created and sustained life. He wanted God's people to come to him to ask for rain when God had always provided. Satan is up to the same tricks today as he was thousands of years ago.

List a few of the ways the world around us claims to be the source of freedom, love, safety, happiness, or rest apart from God.

Elijah must have been ready for God to do something when he confronted the king. Did he imagine Ahab returning his allegiance to God on the spot? Maybe he hadn't thought much past what God had told him to do. I wonder if he was surprised when God whispered, while Elijah still seemed to be standing before Ahab, "Run."

God led him to the desert, where he provided water and bread and meat, the nutrients of life. He gave them daily through a river and ravens. It must have been small amounts that the birds were able to carry. Don't we wish God would send donkeys carrying giant bundles of what we need, instead? It is hard to be daily dependent, waiting hungrily for the next gift. (Elijah was fed morning and night.) It's hard to trust that God is meeting our needs, especially when we feel like we're holding on by a thread. And then, the creek dried up. Even Elijah was not untouched by the punishment of the drought.

Has God ever provided for you in a way that felt like a miracle? When?

Has God's provision to you ever dried up? What happened next?

REFLECTION: ROCKY TIMES

In 1 Kings 17:7 we read that "some time later the brook dried up because there had been no rain in the land." And a dry creek—no water—meant that it was time for Elijah to move beyond bird crumbs. Just because a creek is dry doesn't mean that God's goodness has dried up. Sometimes dry creeks are a gift.

I've sat with many friends staring at situations that felt like dry creek beds, and I've even recently stared down my own. The job, the relationship, or the dream that had felt like such a life-giving provision from God had slowed to a trickle or had become just rocks and mud. It is hard to say goodbye, break camp, and leave, and it's difficult to imagine that there is an-other life somewhere beyond the place we know. God knows it is even harder to leave flowing water. I'm learning to set aside room in my imagination for what he might have beyond where I am today, receiving the grace of goodbye.

> God knows it is even harder to leave flowing water.

I know you've also sat beside your own creeks and probably even had to leave a few. Sometimes the brokenness of our world scorches our beautiful places, but not always. Write on the dry creek-bed stones in this graphic any times you can think of where it felt like something good was taken away but it might have been God's invitation to move on.

What creek are you sitting beside relationally, professionally, or personally? Is there any water level you have been watching carefully? Consider whether anything in your life has been a source of God's goodness or provision in the past but is currently beginning to change or feel dry. Consider writing it on an actual rock with a Sharpie pen. Then ask God if it's time to reinvest or revive that thing, or if it's time to leave it behind.

Dry creek-bed stones

DAY 2 Read 1 Kings 17:8-16

When I was still in Bible college, my friend Beth and I opted to do our student teaching internships in a small missionary school. I showed up in a foreign country for a three-month assignment with seventy-two dollars in my pocket, and Beth was in the same boat. She and I would pray each morning for God to provide, and it was a ridiculous adventure waiting to see what he would do. We would be invited to homes for dinner and scavenged church potlucks; once a stranger handed us a full bag of groceries. Some days we only had a slice of toast for dinner and went to bed with full hearts and grumbly tummies; other times we would bask in that day's miracles of abundance.

While Elijah sat alone by the brook, eating the scraps from ravens, the rest of the country felt the devastation of the drought. Now Elijah had moved outside of Israel into the heart of Baal-worship territory. We often refer to the woman in the story as a poor widow, but we'll see that she had a house with an upper room. So it's likely that before the drought or the death of her husband she was not poor at all. But she's lost just about everything now and is preparing for the end.

Elijah tells her not to be afraid. He makes a promise that the God of Israel will provide for her. She's probably heard of Yahweh, but being immersed in the culture of her city, she almost certainly worshiped Baal. Her rain god hasn't given any rain. The soil and her husband are dead; she and her son will soon die. Can she trust the God of Israel to be the God of life?

She trusts God's promise with a faith and hope that God's own king of Israel lacked. She feeds Elijah first, giving away her last meal, sacrificing her child's last comfort, and surrendering to God all she has.

Elijah tells the widow not to be afraid. What are you afraid that God won't provide for you?

God provided enough food for the woman, her son, and Elijah; there was food every day. He kept his promises. Still, it was the same kitchen jar as before. There was no stockpile of oil. It was a daily act of faith to tip the oil jar forward and trust that God's promises hadn't run dry.

What does daily dependence on God look like for you right now?

REFLECTION: BREATH PRAYER

Breathe in, breathe out. There are many ways to pray, and breath prayer is a beautiful way to pray in a moment. It takes around eight seconds, and you can use it as the beginning of a more extended prayer or on its own throughout the day, especially if there is something you want to remember.

Breath prayer is a four-second inhale followed by a four-second exhale. Repeat up to three times, or consider repeating it at scheduled intervals.

You choose your prayer ahead of time, and in the moment you need it, you can pause and breathe the prayer in and out. It might be a phrase of Scripture, a truth about God, or a request you are bringing to God. Here are a few of my favorites if you want to try them:

A Prayer for When My Needs Feel Big

My God will supply *(Breathe in)*

all my needs. *(Breathe out)**

*Philippians 4:19

A Prayer of Worship

You are good *(Breathe in)*

all the time. *(Breathe out)*

A Prayer for Awareness

Help me trust *(Breathe in)*

that you are here. *(Breathe out)*

Or make your own:

_____

(Breathe in)

_____

(Breathe out)

Allow your prayer to come from your breath today as you remember (1 Thessalonians 5:17).

Wow. Did you just read that? A boy was dead and came back to life when Elijah begged God for his life! If you've been reading the Bible for a while, you might miss how crazy this is. We've been celebrating Easter and Jesus' resurrection for thousands of years, but resurrection from the dead is not normal! This boy being dead and then alive again is the first miracle of resurrection we read in the Bible. Elijah is asking God for something that has never happened before. How did he even imagine it as a possibility? While resurrection from the dead is extremely rare, this miracle makes me wonder if I truly believe *anything* is possible through God.

Have you ever seen a big or small miracle?

Death and life are battling in these first three stories of Elijah's appearance in Israel. First, there's Ahab's choice between sustained life with God or drought and death without God. Then, there's the death that the drought brings and how God's "just enough" provisions for life sustain even through the darkest times. Now death has come, and the power of God to give life will explode on the scene. Life wins.

The death comes as a shock. The boy, his mother, and Elijah live daily under God's miraculous provision through a flour jar and an oil jug that never run dry. They are reminded of God's blessing as they make their bread every morning and afternoon. So how could something so horrible happen if God is with them, saving and protecting them? The widow automatically interprets her son's death as punishment by God for the sins of her past and assumes his messenger Elijah had something to do with it (1 Kings 17:18). Her guilt and shame are awakened by fear and grief, and instead of running to the God who brought her back to life from the brink of starvation, she pushes God and Elijah away.

When something terrible happens, do you find it easier to blame yourself, others, and God or to rely on God and others?

Sometimes death is the backdrop to God's power of life, the first step of resurrection.

How has God's faithfulness (his loyal kindness) unfolded in unexpected ways in your life?

REFLECTION: A SONG TO REMEMBER

The widow of incredible faith woke every morning to find a full oil jug. Without fail, God provided for her and nursed her and her son back to health.

> There is no loss we can suffer that can separate us from the goodness of God.

As soon as tragedy struck, though, she (like many of us) instantly forgot God's faithfulness to her. *There is no loss we can suffer that can separate us from the goodness of God.* If we want to remember that when it counts, we must rehearse that truth while things are good. For centuries people have been reminding themselves of God's faithfulness through the Psalms and their own stories. It is too easy to let our experience of loss define who God is, too easy to blame the giver of life when the evil one attacks with death, destruction, and pain.

Great is Thy Faithfulness

Thomas O. Chisholm   *William M. Runyan*

1. Great is Thy faith-ful-ness, O God my Fa-ther, There is no shad-ow of
2. Sum-mer and win-ter, and spring-time and har-vest, Sun, moon and stars in their
3. Par-don for sin and a peace that en-dur-eth, Thy own dear presence to

turn-ing with Thee; Thou chang-est not, Thy com-pas-sions they fail not;
cours-es a-bove Join with all na-ture in man-i-fold wit-ness
cheer and to guide; Strength for to-day and bright hope for to-mor-row,

Chorus

As Thou hast been Thou for-ev-er wilt be.
To Thy great faith-ful-ness, mer-cy and love. Great is Thy faith-ful-ness!
Bless-ings all mine, with ten thou-sand be-side!

Great is Thy faith-ful-ness! Morn-ing by morn-ing new mer-cies I see; All I have

need-ed Thy hand hath pro-vid-ed— Great is Thy faith-ful-ness, Lord, un-to me!

Loss and hopelessness too often have shaped my imagination of God's goodness. Instead I want my remembrance of his faithfulness—my hope for his rescue—to shape my understanding of the power that evil and suffering have *and don't have* in my life.

How could remembering God's faithfulness to a grieving widow, to generations of millions of people, and to us change the way we pray?

Let the words of this beautiful hymn be sung over you. You might want to find it on your favorite music platform for listening. The lyrics are on the previous page for you to follow as you listen. Imagine churches in the Great Depression singing it together, husbands right now singing it over their wives as they lie in a hospital bed, and Christians around the world singing in the midst of hardship or celebration. When you are ready to join the testimony, sing along.

DAY 4

PRAYER: HEALING PRAYER

We are all surrounded by people who need God's provision, healing, and resurrection. Still, when it comes to praying for healing for someone, I can't escape the echoes of the confident prayers that others proclaimed boldly in my dad's hospital room.

I have lived long enough to know that healing doesn't always come when I pray, and so have you. So it's healthy to take a moment to understand what we hold from our own stories as we pray for those who are sick and hurting.

Have you seen God answer a prayer for healing? What have you learned to expect?

The place I find myself coming back to is that if the world were as God designed it, cancer and other illnesses would not exist. I'm praying in agreement with God's desire to heal the sick. Our world is aching, still waiting for God to heal it and make it look more like heaven. My dad couldn't find his healing here, but God was able to make his brain whole after death. If I don't see the healing I pray for now, I can still celebrate that God's total healing is the reality of heaven. Even in the vulnerable tension between my desire for healing in this life and uncertainty of what God will do, I can keep my eyes alert for what he is doing. The way his goodness appears right where we are in the terrible waiting. Oh, heaven, please break through!

Is there healing that you want for yourself? For others?

Some of the things that help me pray for healing with hope instead of skepticism:

- Not being alone. Inviting others to pray with me, even when it feels vulnerable.
- Starting with worship. Remembering how great, kind, and aware God is.
- Spending time reading stories of Jesus healing others reminds me that God can, does, and will heal—even now. (For example, read Mark 2:1-12; Luke 8:43-48; John 5:1-9.)

- Being honest as I pray about my own fear and equally honest about my desires.

- Keeping a list of "Was that you, God?" coincidences and kindnesses while waiting.

Where can you boldly pray for heaven to break into your reality? Into the experience of others? God, please . . .

DAY 5

PRACTICE: LAMENT

In the face of great loss, the widow and Elijah both cried out to God. Most of us have grief and pain in our lives that we never fully process. My grief kept me from looking God in the eyes for a while, and I was very distant or silent in my prayers. Reading the Psalms, I realized that disappointment, anger, and grief are excellent starting points for prayer. I just hadn't learned to pray that way yet.

It's comforting to know that for thousands of years, God's people have struggled to understand his goodness, power, and justice in the presence of pain, threats, and unnecessary suffering. Made in the image of God, human hearts have burned in defiance at injustice and the triumph of evil for centuries. In response, they wrote songs of lament—prayers that expressed grief and hope simultaneously.

Psalm 23 portrays a good shepherd who guides and protects his sheep. In Psalm 74:1, though, the community asks, "O God, why do you cast us off forever? Why does your anger smoke against the sheep of your pasture?" (ESV). The lament psalms are fearless and unashamed in their honest expressions of pain, betrayal, abandonment, fear, anxiety, or confusion.

Jesus taught his disciples to pray, and he showed them how to lament as he repeated the words of Psalm 22 on the cross.

Lament psalms usually have four parts, although they are not formulaic in the way they order or include these elements:

- *The cry.* Naming the enemy or naming the pain.

- *The ask.* Calling on God for help.

- *The hopeful expectation.* Expressing faith that God can and will help.

- *The celebration.* Celebrating God's character and care.

WRITE YOUR OWN PSALM OF LAMENT

Think of a time recently when you were overwhelmed by a complex memory or intense, negative emotion like anger, fear, jealousy, anxiety, insecurity, helplessness, or rejection. Take courage as you revisit that time. Did you talk to God about it at the moment? Instead, you may have chosen to avoid, escape, or minimize the confrontation, which is a natural human response. Take the chance to talk to God now.

As you write your lament psalm, remember the features of lament prayers from those who came before us:

- *Laments are prayed to God.* God is a safe person to talk to. He will listen to your complaint, confusion, or accusation with compassion. He will not judge you for complaining, and he also has the power to help as well as wisdom about the bigger picture.

- *Laments are prayed alone and together.* This is a personal journaling exercise, but you don't need to carry your pain alone. Instead, find the courage to trust a friend, mentor, or therapist with the grief you are holding before God.

- *Laments are prayed to a God who understands suffering.* Our first instinct is to fear that our faith is small, worry that our disappointment or anger with God will burn the bridge between us, or decide that if God didn't protect us from suffering we can't trust him to help us through it. The opposite is true; we should expect God's empathy and confidently approach him for help in our weaknesses.

For we do not have a high priest who is unable to empathize with our weaknesses, but we have one who has been tempted in every way, just as we are—yet he did not sin. Let us then approach God's throne of grace with confidence, so that we may receive mercy and find grace to help us in our time of need. (Hebrews 4:15-16)

- *Lament psalms express both pain and praise.* Almost all lament psalms are dynamic; they aren't afraid to name evil, fear, shame, or sadness, but they don't stay there. They declare God's faithfulness and praise him even before resolution comes, bringing praise into the pain. The unseen force that pulls the brokenhearted toward hope is a meditation on the kindness and power of God, especially any hint that God has seen, heard, or answered their prayer. Lamenting permits us to share our agony with God as we expectantly watch and wait for his goodness to break into the cold, hopeless loneliness of the dark.

LAMENT TITLE:

DATE:

THE CRY—*naming the enemy or naming the pain.*

THE ASK—*calling on God for help.*

THE HOPEFUL EXPECTATION—*expressing faith that God can and will help.*

THE CELEBRATION—*celebrating God's character and care.*

Allow your lament psalm to rest. Return to it tomorrow and read it aloud as a prayer to God. Allow God to receive your cry. Notice him listening.

> You keep track of all my sorrows.
> You have collected all my tears in your bottle.
> You have recorded each one in your book. (Psalm 56:8 NLT)

WEEK 3

TRUSTING GOD
TO PROVIDE

Give us this day our daily bread. (Part 1)

To pray is to accept that we are, and always will be,
wholly dependent on God for everything.

TIMOTHY KELLER

———

God will provide what we need, whether he has made specific promises or not.

SUMMARY OF WEEK TWO

- The way God was providing for Elijah unexpectedly changed.
- Elijah learned to trust God to provide what he needed one day at a time.
- While Elijah was feeling cared for by God, tragedy struck. Was God with him or not?

What stood out to you last week? Was there something from your study, your life, or your conversations with God that you would like to share?

Notes

- Moses intercedes for God to make a way.

- Elijah intercedes for the people to follow God's way.

- Jesus intercedes *as* the way.

DISCUSS

1. What needs or wants are you praying for right now?

2. Sometimes we talk about being "burdened" by our own needs or the needs of others—that is, feeling the weight of those prayers. If you had a backpack holding the burden of your prayer requests to God, how much would you say it weighs?

3. How do you hold on to the hope that God is good even when he is not giving you what you need?

ALL TOGETHER: SPIRITUAL JOURNEY MAPPING

Materials: Paper and pens or pencils (optional: markers, colored pencils)

Elijah went from the king's presence to the obscurity of the desert to the home of a pagan widow. He experienced the highs of God's provision, the lows of watching a boy die, and the confusion of thinking God had placed him somewhere and then watching that place dry up. Elijah's journey is far from over. This week he'll be a part of a colossal divine intervention. Elijah's journey is anything but "up and to the right." It twists and turns and spirals. Sometimes God feels big and powerful and close; other times, it seems as if God has turned his attention elsewhere.

All of us are on a spiritual journey. We can be so focused on where we are going that we forget to remember where we have been. Spiritual journey mapping can help us.

Drawing a life map. Here are two kinds of maps that might be helpful as you draw your own life map: timeline and typographical mapping. If you have your own way of mapping milestones—go for it!

TIMELINE LIFE MAPPING

- Turn your paper to a landscape orientation and draw a line on the bottom of your page. If you're a math person, this is your *x* axis.
- Label some notches to note a timeline. You might start on the day you were born and go up to today, or start the timeline at the beginning of a more recent milestone.
- Draw a vertical line, or *y* axis, and notch with a scale of 0-10, 10 being at the top of your paper. The number 10 is the absolute best, and 0 is the absolute worst.

- Plot some key events on your timeline. Your happiest, most satisfied, meaningful experiences will be near the top of the paper, and disappointments, losses, embarrassments, grief, or sadness near the bottom.
- Label the points and connect them with a line.
- Add symbols or notes for important people, lessons learned, memorable words or phrases that were said to you and stuck, and any time you thought God might have shown up.
- What were your goals along the way? Your fears?

Optional: If the linear concept doesn't work for you, feel free to mark off a path—however winding it might be—and add all those same elements (symbols, words, names, goals, etc.) that help you tell your story.

Here is an example of what Elijah's map might have looked like:

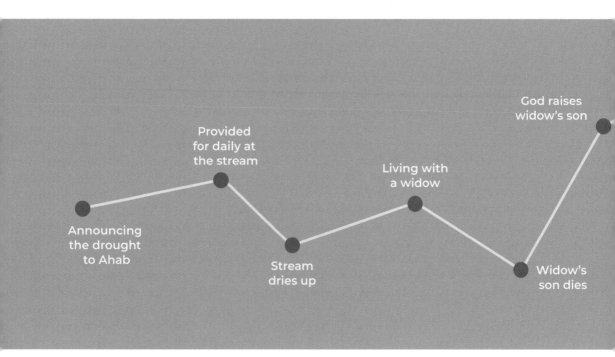

MAP REFLECTIONS

1. Is there anything or anyone you'd want to thank God for?

2. Are there any points where it seems God could have been with you, guiding you? Did you realize it at the time?

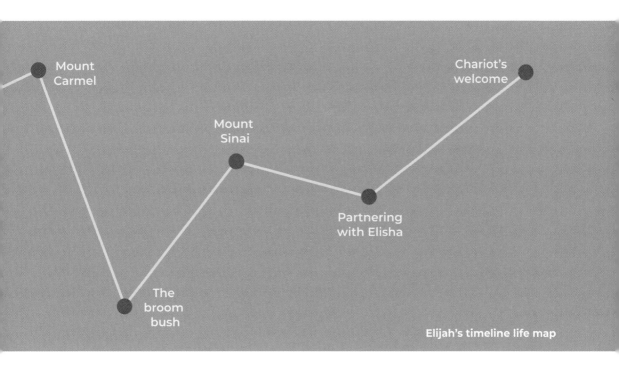

Elijah's timeline life map

Mount Carmel

Mount Sinai

The broom bush

Partnering with Elisha

Chariot's welcome

3. Our life and faith are constantly changing. Sometimes God seems close and things are good, while other times, it can be a battle to believe God cares or even exists. How do your current or past spiritual seasons affect how you pray?

MAP SHARING

Share your map with your small group or a friend if you feel comfortable. You don't have to share every point on the map—you can leave blank spaces if you like.

As everyone shares, honor one another's stories with gratitude, compassion, and suspended judgment. Avoid giving advice or opinions about the events on one another's maps. Please take a moment to note something beautiful you saw or heard on each person's map or how their current life reflects their story. What an honor to hold another person's story! What a sacred joy to show up as your full self and rest in belonging!

PRAY TOGETHER: BROKEN ROAD

After reflecting and sharing your map, break into partners or stay as a large group and share.

1. Where did God's goodness break into your story?

2. Where does it still hurt?

Did you notice something about your story you can celebrate? Is there something from your past that doesn't feel healed or something you want badly for your future? We can pray about these real things as we share this stretch of our spiritual journey together.

SOLO STUDY

Some easy adjustments if you are on this journey with us, but without a group:

- Draw your own life map. What stands out to you?

- Is there a person on your map that you want to reach out to? This week you might say thank you or I'm sorry or I forgive you to them.

Obadiah was loyal to God. Within the palace of Ahab and Jezebel, with its anti-God rhetoric, persecution of prophets, temptations, and pressure to participate in worship or deference to Baal dozens of times throughout the day, Obadiah remained faithful to God. He had a significant role of leadership and power within a corrupt government, and he used all his privilege and influence to protect the weak, to feed and hide the prophets of God.

Considering the threat to the prophets of God, Obadiah likely prayed in secret most of the time. Waiting, praying, and hoping that God would judge the evil in the palace, he must have anticipated the day the people could return to openly worshiping their Lord.

When we pray for God to move, his miracles won't always come in a quick flash of glory (but they sometimes do!). The drought in Israel has been years in the making, the physical hunger and thirst of Israel are palpable. Elijah won't just pray one big prayer alone later in this chapter; the cries of God's faithful people have already been pounding on the door of heaven—from the prophets' cave, from Obadiah's closet, from unknown corners of widows' houses. God is listening.

Obadiah can only trust that God is listening; all signs point to Ahab still being completely in command. On the brink of an incredible demonstration that God is far more powerful than the king or his false prophets, Obadiah stutters in fear. He gives five full verses of excuses why he cannot obey Elijah's request from God, and they boil down to this—"Ahab will kill me." Elijah responds with as strong of reassurance that he can offer, "As the LORD Almighty lives, whom I serve, I will surely present myself to Ahab today."

The first time I read Obadiah's monologue, I thought his excuses were valid on the surface but betrayed his lack of trust in God's protection. They sounded like excuses and justifications, reasons he couldn't or wouldn't obey. I'm pretty sure the reason I judged him so harshly is that it mirrors a trait in myself I dislike. I'll do *a lot* of things for God without even being asked, but if he asks me to do something I don't want to do, I usually have a reason why I can't.

That's why the first three words of verse 16 strike me: "So Obadiah went." He went scared. He went with nothing but the promise of God and Elijah. That courage and faith in the face of real and true danger didn't come from nowhere.

It was born from years of small, faithful actions in his palace life—key moments of practicing risk on behalf of God's prophets and accumulating stories of God's protection. Years of prayers in the dark. Years of saying yes to God in the small things so he could say yes when it counted.

How have you been faithful to God in small or big ways during your ordinary days this week?

Have you ever said yes to God even though you feared what could happen?

REFLECTION: HORIZON PRAYERS

Obadiah must have felt as if his prayers for God to move on behalf of Israel were filed in a basement of heaven. Prayer after prayer, cry after cry, and nothing seemed to change in the palace—maybe it seemed to get worse?

Is there anything or anyone you stopped praying for because it seemed God wasn't moving?

Take a moment to pray. Leave yourself a note in a place you see often, or schedule a recurring meeting on your calendar to pray. After all those years of prayer, Obadiah had no reason to know that he was hours away from God's miraculous show of power. We have no idea how close we are either.

Baal was more than an idol made of stone; he was a spiritual being that used his power to reward people who worshiped him. While his power wasn't as great as God's, Baal encouraged transactional worship—you gave him something, he gave you something in return.

Baal was one of the chief challengers of God in the Old Testament, and the Canaanites and Egyptians worshiped him within a pantheon of spiritual beings. His name means "lord." He called himself "king of the gods" as well as the god of fertility or life. The God of Israel, Yahweh, is Lord of lords, King of heaven. The Creator God who generates life. Baal claimed to be all those things himself and offered himself to humanity as an alternative to God.

During this drought, Baal—the supposed god of rain, fertility, storms, and clouds—had failed to produce rain when God had cut it off. His worshipers had ways to explain this. During times of drought, they believed Baal had fought another god in the pantheon (usually Mot, the god of sterility and death) and been defeated, but only for a time. Then, after seven years, he would battle again and hopefully win, bringing fertility again.

It's unclear how long the drought had been going on; James taught that it was three and a half years (James 5:17). Some people may still have been expecting Baal to be up for another battle, ready to pull them out of Mot's grip. This display on Carmel was a chance for Baal to take credit for ending the drought and usher in his victorious season of rain and fertility. But Baal never showed up. Had Mot won one again? Would it be another seven years of drought? The Israelites who had bought into the story of Baal had no place for God in it. God's people were watching the skies for Baal and Mot and had seemingly forgotten God himself. Like Israel, I can tell myself stories about why things are happening that are disconnected from the story of God that I claim defines me.

In that moment, Elijah prayed for three things (1 Kings 18:36-37):

1. "Let it be known today that you are_____

2. and that I am _____ . . .

3. so these people will know that you, LORD, are God, and that_____

_____."

Elijah prayed earnestly: *Hear my prayer.*

- That people would know God is the King of the gods, not Baal.

- That people would see past Elijah and look at God and his power.

- That people would recognize God as LORD, not Baal who named himself "lord," and that they would repent and worship God again.

The fire from heaven was not merely a contest of which God could put on a better show—God is so much more powerful than Baal, it was hardly a contest. It wasn't a question of if God could send fire—but whether he would. The people were crying out to heaven to see who would answer, who was paying attention, whose power and presence they could rely on. The silenced sky of Baal, god of lightning, and the awe-inspiring fire of God that illuminated the heavens invited Israel back into their story that they had forgotten. God didn't need to battle Baal to prove his power, he agreed to the challenge to win back the hearts of his people. Only one Creator, God, created, designed, and sustains life. Above all other spiritual beings, he alone is Lord and King of the heavens. Counterfeit gods—money, power, achievement, sex, and beauty all line up among others in the pantheon—will always promise to give me what only God gives: *life.*

Elijah prayed
earnestly:
Hear my prayer.

I've heard people say that if we have enough faith or big enough prayers, we can call down fire from heaven just as Elijah did. I think the invitation has always been slightly different—not to be the one who conjures fire but to be the one who receives it. The one who can look at the blank sky and see clearly that the promises of ambition, hustle, success, power, and social status never come when I call. To turn my heart back to the only God who has ever listened when I cry, "Lord, hear my prayer."

What things are you tempted to turn to for a fulfilled life?

REFLECTION: MEMORIZATION

One of the best ways to meditate on Scripture is to memorize it. Letting God's Word roll around in our minds as our days unfold before us brings his words to life. It invites the wisdom, questions, and tensions of the Bible to step into the light of day, off the thin pages and into the space where we live. Part of prayer is making space to listen, and letting God's words speak into our life is an easy way to start.

One of the verses from today's passage sounded like an underline-worthy, meme-able quote the first time I read it—but it changed my life when I made space for it in my mind and brought it into the decisions I was wrestling with.

> Elijah went before the people and said, "How long will you waver between two opinions? If the LORD is God, follow him; but if Baal is God, follow him."
> *But the people said nothing.* (1 Kings 18:21, emphasis added)

After recognizing Baal as a counterfeit god who claims to give what only God can—life, purpose, meaning, belonging, security, and the rest—it became easier to substitute his name.

If success is a god that can provide for all your needs, chase that.

If being good-looking is the pathway to love and opportunity, chase that.

If money is god and makes a good life possible, then choose the job that makes the most. Just wait to see if the promised joy, security, sense of purpose, and connection follow.

I know who I'm following. I'm not going to let the fake promisers lie to me anymore. There are lots of good things that I can enjoy without depending on them to satisfy me.

One of my favorite ways to memorize Scripture is to keep the first letter of each word as a prompt to help while repeating, meditating on, and memorizing a verse.

Check out this graphic; look at the letters and repeat the verse—1 Kings 18:21:

> "How long will you waver between two opinions? If the LORD
>   is God, follow him; but if Baal is God, follow him."
>   But the people said nothing.

Find a digital copy of this image at www.lizditty.com /prayer. You can use it as the lock screen or wallpaper on your phone. Try to recite the verse every morning and night, and as you go through the day. Think of which counterfeit promiser is trying to gain your following—and what it looks like to follow the one true God of life.

DAY 3 — *Read 1 Kings 18:41-46*

Elijah does not look toward the horizon; he looks to God. Kneeling, with his head bowed, he sends his assistant to look at the sky to see if God's promise has come.

Nothing.

God promised to send rain. Elijah promised Ahab that God would send rain. Elijah's life is on the line for God's promise, and even the recent fire from heaven does not fill Elijah with overconfidence or nonchalance. He is on his knees, praying, "God, where is your promise?"

Look again.

We have all learned to read our skies. We know the cottony clouds that tell us fair weather is ahead and the ominous, dark clouds that mean rain is coming. But how many of us are staring at blue skies, waiting for rain? I hear people say that there are no singles in their circles, no open places for promotion, no colleges that will accept them, no hope for a child, or no homes they can afford. I see Elijah's assistant running to the mountaintop. He's breathless, straining his eyes, afraid to return to the prophet with no sign, no hope, no change from the years of drought, dry throats, and cracked ground.

Nothing.

Elijah's head must be tired now; his forehead may be touching the ground beneath his knees. His eyes are on God. He doesn't see the empty sky; he sees the God who has always kept his promises, the God who has defended his reputation, the God who sent ravens with scraps of bread and meat to feed him, the God who was reliable to fill oil in the jar daily, the God who raised a boy from the dead and who just sent fire from heaven. During his times of desperation, Elijah's eyes had been trained to look for God's provision. Yes. This God could bring rain.

Look again.

Nothing.

And this is where my faith begins to show its weakness. Just because God can doesn't mean he will. Do I believe that the God of miracles and fire from heaven hasn't left me?

Look again.

Nothing.

Still, Elijah doggedly keeps his face to the ground, his spirit before the God of heaven. Without any sign of hope, circumstance, connection, or prospect, he asks God to do what God is already planning to do. But it has not been done yet.

Look again.

Nothing.

The waiting is the hardest part, but God repeatedly proves that the waiting isn't something that can be skipped or rushed. On the contrary, it is an essential part of the promise kept, the joy unearthed in the end. When it looks like nothing is happening, something is happening. God is working in you, through you, around you, in ways you cannot always see.

Look again.

Nothing.

Assuming that Elijah is not sending his assistant back the second he returns to him with no news, sending his messenger and waiting for his return seven times was at minimum several hours, maybe even several days or weeks. Some of us have waited for years, even decades, watching the sky for just the right cloud, trying to remember if God ever said it would rain; it seems so long ago now.

Look again.

Is that something? It's so tiny!

Tiny is enough. It is okay to get our hopes up when we've been waiting for a sign. It's okay to expect a rainstorm before the first cloud turns gray. Elijah didn't declare the drought over because of the fire that had just hit Mount Carmel or because of a tiny cloud. He knew the rain was coming because he patiently waited with God in prayer, looking for God's answer. He recognized it instantly when even a hint of it appeared.

What drought-ending rain are you waiting for?

What would it look like to wait with God in prayer?

REFLECTION: VISIO DIVINA

Visio divina is a form of meditation that begins with an image and leads to prayer. These images could be pieces of art or icons, statues, symbols, or even visions. The Bible uses imagery to communicate truths about God or his plans for the world. Throughout history, the church has also created art to retell the realities of the Bible.

Visio divina is a conversation with God where we invite him to look at an image with us. God may illuminate a truth through that image or simply gaze with you to appreciate the beauty or significance of the image with you. We'll practice with a picture of a stormy sky.

First Kings 18:42-43 paints the powerful vision of an empty sky. God has already promised to end the drought (18:1), but the sky is clear and blue. God has won the contest to show that he is above all other gods and idols (18:38-39), but will the God of fire also send rain? Can God's people remember his power from the dry place of scarcity and thirst?

The sky stays empty for so long. Then the smallest wisp of a cloud forms—nothing that looks like rain, but the seed of something that God intends to grow.

Begin your time of visio divina prayer by slowly reading 1 Kings 18:41-45.

Breathe slowly and intentionally.

Invite God to speak to you through the image of a coming rainstorm, "Strength for Us All" by Janine Crum.

Allow your eyes to focus on one element or take in the whole image.

Reflect on the image as you like, or use these prompts if they are helpful:

What small cloud are you waiting to hear news of? What rain (provision, protection, new life) are you waiting for?

What does your sky look like right now? How would you describe the clouds?

Is there anyone watching your sky with you? If not, who could you invite?

What does the sky tell us about who God is or what he is like?

What do you learn about yourself as you stare at the sky?

Allow your eyes to close and reopen them to look at the image again.

Notice God's presence, trust that he is near, and rest.

After a moment, you may articulate a prayer with words or express gratitude to God in whatever way seems natural.

DAY 4

PRAYER: LISTENING PRAYER

When you pray, do you have the same confidence as Elijah that God is listening? Do you ever sense God hearing you or speaking to you? Is there a way, place, or time that you like to pray?

Most of us are easily distracted as we pray. We lose our train of thought quickly. We think of prayer as talking to God, but we're usually just talking at God—rarely pausing to listen for his part of the conversation. We are uncomfortable with silence, and our minds rush to fill it with one of the many other things vying for our attention.

Listening prayer is about sitting in silence, shepherding our attention as it wanders. It takes practice to be comfortable with silence, but small steps can take us far. With practice, we can be satisfied with the presence of God; it can become the sacred space where we most feel like ourselves and most feel at rest. Let's try.

1. Find a quiet place and set a timer for three minutes.

2. Inhale a deep breath. Know that if you are a follower of Jesus, the Spirit of God is within you. Make yourself available to listen.

3. As thoughts and distractions invade your silence, identify them and set them aside. Some people have different visualizing techniques for this. For example, you might visualize the interrupting thoughts like sheep wandering and then gently corral each stray thought into a safe pen to be dealt with later. If this helps you, try it. If not, come up with a better way to release your distractions.

4. Try to maintain a sense of silence and make yourself present, with your full attention on the presence of the Holy Spirit. Listen until the timer goes off.

5. Thank God for his presence and for the grace to become even more aware.

6. Reflect on the most intrusive distractions. Is there a fixation you need to release?

7. Try again tomorrow and see if you can add a minute to the timer each day.

8. Keep trying. These snatches of silence are practice for stillness, awareness, and being ready to receive—they will not always be profound. God's gifts can take many forms, even the silence itself.

PRACTICE: TRACING A LABYRINTH

If you were to walk inside Notre Dame de Chartres in France, you'd find an eleven-circuit labyrinth maze inlaid on the floor, which pilgrims have walked since the 1200s. Walking the circle started as a way to symbolize a pilgrimage to the Holy Land, but over time it became the pilgrimage many would take to meet with God. Just as Elijah ran to a place he knew, where God had been before with Moses, many have come to slowly make their way through a labyrinth expecting to hear from God along their journey.

There are three stages of moving through a labyrinth.

1. **Purgation**—an emptying. As you begin, clear your mind of distracting thoughts. If you are walking outside, consider taking your shoes off. Use your senses and deep breaths to be present in your body in this moment. If you have a question, you can focus on articulating it clearly as you bring it to the center.

2. **Illumination**—a filling. As you approach the center, take a deep breath. Settle into the silence you have cultivated for a time of meditation, listening, and prayer. You might ask your question here. This is your opportunity to receive rest, a word or image, or silence.

3. **Union**—an incorporating. On your walk out, consider how the presence of God or whatever you have received changes your perspective. Resist overanalyzing, and do not be concerned if your expectations are not met. The path is a tool to quiet our minds and lead us to God's presence. The walk in itself is a gift, and receiving takes practice.

Since you are probably not near Notre Dame or another labyrinth, consider tracing this replica with a pen or even your finger, moving slowly and listening carefully.

You could also go on your own pilgrimage, alone or with a friend. You might take a labyrinth hike, and your "walk in" could be a walk out or a walk up. Clear your minds by taking time to listen and process with one another, or tell God all that is racing through your thoughts. Once you get to the top or a turning point, if you are with someone, try to give one another the gift of silence for the first few moments, to reflect, listen, and pray. On the walk back, pray with and for one another. Take this time to encourage each other.

Chartres labyrinth

RECEIVING WHAT GOD PROVIDES

Give us this day our daily bread. (Part 2)

Mental prayer in my opinion is nothing else than an intimate sharing
between friends; it means taking time frequently to be alone with
Him who we know loves us. The important thing is not to think
much but to love much and so do that which best stirs you to love.
Love is not great delight but desire to please God in everything.

SAINT TERESA OF ÁVILA

GROUP SESSION

The things we need from God aren't always miracles. We can also look for the ordinary gifts or kind people in our lives that God provides to strengthen our body, mind, and spirit.

SUMMARY OF WEEK THREE

- Obadiah relied on a history of God's faithfulness.
- Elijah saw a massive sign of God's faithfulness.
- All of Israel enjoyed the gift of God's faithfulness.

What stood out to you last week? Was there something from your study, your life, or your conversations with God that you would like to share?

Notes

- Signs can't convince anyone of anything.

- Signs can't give us the security we crave.

- Signs can't do what silence can.

DISCUSS

1. Are you overwhelmed, exhausted, or burned out?

2. What needs might your body be communicating to you through sleep, energy levels, appetite, or other ways?

3. How do you know whether you have had an encounter with God or your mind is playing tricks on you?

ALL TOGETHER: SPIRITUAL STYLES

Think of the last time God felt real or close, or you felt wonder at the spiritual reality hiding within our physical world. Where were you? What were you doing? Each of us has our own stories and wiring that make it easier for us to connect with God in our own ways—we don't have to pray or spend time with God the way someone else does.

Moving around your group, take turns reading the spiritual styles below aloud. They are similar to the ones that Gary Thomas identified in his book *Sacred Pathways: Discovering Your Soul's Path to God*. Rank the top three that resonate with you. No matter which style you most identify with, you'll probably enjoy connecting with God in a variety of ways.

1. Nature lover. You might feel most at home connecting with God outside. Nothing draws you to wonder and worship like a granite face, the rush of water around a paddle, or a sky full of stars. You might be drawn to physical challenges, time alone, or simply the distraction-free way of being present and away from technology in beautiful places.

2. Sensory spirit. Has a cathedral taken your breath away? Have your eyes wandered to decipher the brilliant colors and designs of stained glass? Do you like the ash of Ash Wednesday being traced on your forehead or the smell of fresh bread at Communion? You may appreciate using all your five senses when you worship, and there could be ways you try to incorporate sensory elements into normally dull environments. For example, while doing this study you might want to play instrumental music on headphones, light a scented candle, or take your book outside to read near the smell of freshly cut grass.

3. Classical. For some of you, formality, history, and tradition draw your souls to the sacred. You appreciate the tried-and-true methods of spiritual disciplines that were developed, practiced, and proven over the centuries. You value the link to the generations of faith that preceded you, or the tie to countless others today through a shared liturgy. Even if this is not your primary style, it can serve as an anchor when contemporary confusion unsteadies your faith.

4. Minimalist. Simplicity may be what speaks loudest to your soul. Stepping away from distractions through silence or solitude revives your soul. Much of your relationship with God feels interior, and you experience him most clearly on your own rather than in a large group or service.

5. Kingdom-come Christian. You are always reminding those around you of the ways our earth groans for God's justice. You take seriously the mission of the church—to make God's kingdom visible until Jesus returns to make everything right, finally. You are sensitive to how the church falls short of its values of equality and generosity. Your faith comes alive when you take God's goodness outside the church walls into the community, and sometimes the pain around you feels too heavy.

6. Helper. Thank you for being the hands, feet, and heart of Christ to so many of us. You are the first one people call for advice or comfort. You are compassionate and feel a strong partnership with God while serving others. You have experienced the Holy Spirit working through and around you in near-miraculous ways and feel drawn to be where the Spirit is healing, helping, and bringing life.

7. Emotional. When the chorus builds, your hands are in the air! You cannot sit still while you worship. You love big experiences that make your heart soar. You love feeling close to God. Joy and celebration come naturally to you. You aren't afraid to let a tear fall. You feel especially drawn to transcendent experiences through art and music.

8. Mindful. Being alone with God is very important to you. You have a close and intimate relationship that you enjoy. You can go for a walk with God and not feel like you are by yourself. You enjoy a deep friendship with God. Your prayer life is very important to you. You love being part of a Christian community, but most of your meaningful experiences with God are while you are thinking about him or with him on your own.

9. Thinking. You love to learn. You are an avid reader and have a stack of books everywhere you spend a lot of time. You can recommend a resource on nearly any topic. You connect with God by researching to explore and understand truth. You are always hungry for fresh knowledge and insight. You connect with people and God around ideas, frameworks, and perspectives. It is important to you that God and his words be represented accurately.

Take a moment to share your assessment results with one another.

1. Were there any surprises?

2. How could being aware of your most intuitive spiritual pathways change the way you pray?

3. How have your spiritual styles changed over time? Why do you think that is?

4. What role have people or relationships had in shaping the way you feel connected to God?

APPLICATION

As you follow the command of Jesus to love God with all your heart, soul, mind, and strength and to love your neighbor as yourself (Mark 12:30-31), it can be helpful to notice in what ways your heart, soul, and mind most intuitively lead you to love.

Your type is not meant to define you, only to guide you.

While it can be helpful to return to God on well-worn paths, it is also worth going out of your way sometimes. Reading Scripture, attending church, or serving the poor may not be what naturally stirs connection for you, but they are all important as you grow to be more like Jesus. You might find someone who lights up with a spiritual style that isn't natural to you, and you can let their joy become contagious to you. Trying something you know will work is great for meeting God, but trying something new can challenge you and shake you out of a rut—so don't get stuck in only one style of moving toward God.

PRAYING TOGETHER: THEMED PRAYER

Whose birthday is next? That person will choose one of the following themes, and everyone who is willing can give a personal prayer request following that theme.

- Relationships/family
- Career
- Health/mental health
- Dreams and goals
- Currently waiting

Once everyone who wants to has asked for prayer, open the time, and anyone can pray for anyone else. If your spiritual pathway has given you an idea of how you want to pray (kneeling, standing, reciting a Scripture verse, singing part of a song), feel free to pray in your own way.

Make a note to pray for your group this week, and connect with them somehow to let them know they have been on your mind.

Some easy adjustments if you are on this journey with us, but without a group:

- Which styles resonated most with you?

- How could you incorporate your preferred style of connecting with God with your study this week?

DAY 1 — Read 1 Kings 18:45–19:9

It rained. In an agrarian society, water is life. After three years of drought, the land was in a severe famine. People were starving, children were dying, desperation drove fear and violence, and the earth was cracked and broken. Then Elijah prayed with his eyes closed, not daring to look, and a little raincloud grew into a rainstorm. For the first time in years, Elijah and those around him felt the heaviness of wet clothes, the goosebumps of damp skin, the tangle of wet hair. Children squealed and ran outside. Everyone looking to heaven, staring at the dark gray, generous sky.

Elijah ran through the storm, so fast that he outpaced the king's chariot. What must it have felt like to be the prophet of Israel? They were God's chosen people, but they had decided to worship other gods instead. Elijah saw the violence and horror of Baal worship and the gross ways the king and queen abused their powers instead of leading God's people. But now. Not only had God decisively won the contest on the top of Mount Carmel, but God was also restoring and blessing the land again with *rain*. Glorious rain! People had no choice but to recognize God's power and provision. Elijah had never run so far, so fast, and so happily. Finally, one nation under God, the way it was supposed to be!

I wonder what plans he was making as he ran toward the palace: Plans for the temple? For himself? He thought he knew the story God was writing and the path he was on. He had waited in the wilderness and hid in a foreign widow's humble home, but God had only been preparing him. He thought this was it—the moment he had turned the country back to God.

But he was wrong.

As Elijah was preparing to declare the victory of Yahweh over Baal at the palace, Queen Jezebel had another announcement to make. She did not acknowledge the defeat of Baal. People say they want signs and miracles, but in the end, many people only want their own way. Jezebel orders Elijah dead, so Elijah runs for his life.

Think of a time you felt so sure God was doing something, and then it turned out his plan was completely different. How did that feel at the time? What do you think about it now?

Elijah quits, disappointed in God and unsure of what to do with that disappointment. He leaves his assistant safe in another town to find other employment, and he wanders out into the desert. Elijah collapses under the weight of his anxiety, depression, anger, and fear, and asks God to take his life. The only escape he can imagine from the darkness he feels is death. "I have had enough, Lord," he says. "Take my life; I am no better than my ancestors" (1 Kings 19:4). Elijah isn't being dramatic; he expects God to end his life.

Burnout is real.

If faith, prayer, or spiritual connection with God could make you exempt from depression, anxiety, or suicidal ideation, Elijah would not have struggled. Instead, he's a patron prophet for the rest of us.

I've gone through two challenging seasons of diagnosed depression. I experienced postpartum depression and anxiety (PPDA) after giving birth and major depressive disorder (MDD) in middle age. Like Elijah, in both cases I had experienced an incredible high point and then floundered in my disappointment afterward. Elijah appears to have what we would call situational depression, although our narrator doesn't use technical terms. When I was diagnosed with clinical depression, I sat with Elijah under the wide-reaching leafy branches of the broom tree. I wondered if he knew what it was like to drown.

> If faith, prayer, or spiritual connection with God could make you exempt from depression, anxiety, or suicidal ideation, Elijah would not have struggled.

No one was trying to kill me when I was depressed, but panic still convinced my heart to race and my mind to fear I was in imminent danger. I felt as if I was treading water frantically, and depression was reaching up from deep below grabbing my ankles. If I didn't swim hard enough for even a moment, I'd plunge beneath the surface, screaming, gasping for air, only inhaling water, scrambling to swim back toward the sky. I was fighting hardest to keep my head above water and not let anyone know how hard I was working to do what they all seemed to do effortlessly, floating calmly. I was overwhelmed, exhausted, and all the pretending to be okay made me lonely. I was so much more than sad. I asked God to help, over and over. Release me from this grip! Cut the chains to this thing dragging me away from my kids, my husband, my friends, my goals, and myself.

Really, my prayer was for God to cure me without anyone having to know, just between him and me. Sitting with Elijah taught me to look up and see the angels: the friends inviting me on hikes, the incredible counseling center near my home, the doctor who knew what my body needed, the patience of my husband learning to support me in a new way. God answers prayers through his people, his church, and even some surprising messengers. He knows how intricately connected our soul is to our body, and because he loves us, he cares for both.

How might your body receive God's gifts of food, rest, or movement to help your spirit heal?

God sends an angel to feed his prophet twice, and Elijah needs sleep. Otherwise, as the angel warns him, "The journey is too much for you." Is your journey too much for you?

Does anything make you want to run, hide, or quit? How is your sleep?

Could there be an angel you haven't noticed that is available to help your body or mind heal? Ask God to draw attention to a helper he might have sent for you.

God's tenderness always finds me as it finds Elijah, and I remember that I am much more prone to quit on God than he is to quit on me.

REFLECTION: A PRAYER FOR US TODAY

If you are discouraged, nestle in a cozy place, grab a snack, and receive this prayer today.

> God, you are the One who doesn't only wait for us on the mountaintops but also meets us in the valleys. The One who sees us when we are exhausted, on the run, and ready to quit. You are the giver of bread, sleep, and comfort. I need you to nurse me back to joy.
>
> I'm sorry for how I've wanted to make your fire and power the fuel for my success and agenda. I'm holding disappointment that I'm afraid to explore fully, and it's making my soul ache. I'm grieving the imagined future that I lost, with nothing to hold or bury.
>
> God, you are the mother hen who holds her chicks beneath a warm, tufted wing. Would you find me? Feed me. Wrap your arm around me— where I am wanted, safe, and close enough to hear your heartbeat. A place where I don't need to manage everyone and everything around me but only be still. God, I'm tired, and I want to be held. Hold us, please. Amen.

DAY 2   *Read 1 Kings 19:9-18*

The journey Elijah is about to take to the mountain of God, to the caves at Mount Sinai, is a journey not only to a place but to a moment. It's an encounter with God where past, present, and future collide.

Elijah knows the significance of the mountain he stands on. It's the same mountain where Moses saw the burning bush, where Moses received the Ten Commandments, and where Moses met God again to witness God's glory pass by him. Just as Moses wandered for forty years in the surrounding desert, Elijah journeys for forty days to Mount Sinai, but that won't be the last of the ways Elijah's encounter with God will remind us of Moses meeting with God in this same place in Exodus 19 and 33.

We start in the present moment. As Elijah arrives on Mount Sinai, God greets him with a simple question: "What are you doing here, Elijah?" (verse 9).

Notice Elijah's response (verse 10).

Elijah comes to God with undeniable proof that he has not been good: *your prophets were put to death by the sword.* As if to say, "You didn't protect them, and you haven't protected me, or I wouldn't be running for my life."

Elijah's grief comes to God as accusation, not lament. (Look back on Day 5 from Week 2 to remind you of the lament psalms.) If Elijah had lamented the injustice of the murder of God's prophets, his anger would have been directed at Ahab, at Baal, at the evil that hovered over his (and our) world like a dark cloud. He could have cried out to God and appealed to God's own sense of justice and sorrow at how his prophets had been treated. He could have remembered God's goodness and power and pleaded with him to intervene. But he doesn't do that. He's too lonely and overwhelmed by despair. He doesn't really pray the "right" prayer, but God hears messy prayers and loves messy people—which is good news for all of us.

When has your heart dared to whisper, "God, you failed me before . . . and I've seen you fail others . . . so what can I expect from you now?"

The answer to Elijah's questions, and ours, isn't a sign or a promise. Instead, it is an encounter—an experience of God's presence. As Elijah stood at the entrance to the cave, waiting to encounter God, there was:

- "A great and powerful wind . . . but the LORD was not in the wind."
- "An earthquake, but the LORD was not in the earthquake."
- "A fire, but the LORD was not in the fire."
- But then there is a soft wind, a gentle whisper. And it's God.

In Hebrew, the still, small voice or gentle wind is *qol demamah daqqah*, translated as "the sound of thin silence." God's glory is described in two ways, using light and weight. Can you remember a time when everything suddenly got very quiet? When there was a whole room waiting for what would happen next or what someone would say? Those are thick, heavy silences. They loom darkly with a buzz of anxiety. They feel significant and charged. There's nothing more disappointing than trying to be with God but feeling nothingness instead. Emptiness. Thin silence.

> There's nothing more disappointing than trying to be with God but feeling nothingness instead.

The fire, earthquake, and mighty wind aren't just for show—they are very strategically for comparison. Elijah is standing on the same mountain where Moses met God in Exodus 19. Turn back to see Moses encountering God's presence during the time he received the Ten Commandments and compare it with Elijah's encounter:

> Mount Sinai was covered with smoke because the LORD descended on it in fire. The smoke billowed up from it like smoke from a furnace, and the whole mountain trembled violently. As the sound of the trumpet grew louder and louder, Moses spoke and the voice of God answered him. (Exodus 19:18-19)

Circle Y for Yes or N for No to indicate if the parallel elements contained the power and presence of God:

GOD'S PRESENCE

1 Kings 19:9-18	God?	Exodus 19:18-19	God?
A great and powerful wind	Y | N	Billowing smoke	Y | N
An earthquake	Y | N	The mountain trembled violently	Y | N
A fire	Y | N		
		A fire	Y | N
A gentle whisper	Y | N	The sound of a loud trumpet	Y | N

This triad of wind, earthquake, and fire marks God's presence in multiple places in the Bible, including the Psalms and Isaiah. Elijah had every reason to expect God to appear in one of those forms, but God's presence came to him differently. God is unchanging while still making all things new. There are ways that we expect God to speak to us. God's words in the Bible and prayer are foundational and essential—like fire and wind when it comes to recognizing God's presence. But notice that Elijah, who has likely come to the mountain to re-create the experience Moses had with God, is met by God in a new way. God is not in the fire and wind and earthquake this time, and instead of a trumpet that gets louder and louder, he speaks in a quieter and quieter whisper. He meets Elijah in an unexpected way, which is exactly what he needs.

Have you ever tried to hear God's voice in the way others described it but not shared their experience? Have you ever heard God's voice in a way that you didn't expect?

REFLECTION: CAVE WHISPER JOURNALING

Writing our thoughts, prayers, and feelings down not only preserves them but also enhances them. Our prayers are no longer fleeting, easily distracted thoughts when we journal. Instead, they are words that we see on paper, letters that our hands move to make, and pressure we feel on the page with our pen. If you are new to journaling, try using these prompts from Elijah's experience in the cave to reflect and pray.

Take time to move toward God. Elijah ran to the mountain of God, where he knew there was a history of God's presence. Where have you learned to find God? Through worship and praise? Nature? In conversations with other people? While serving the poor? During quiet times of reading and prayer? Choose a location or activity that helps you feel connected to God, and prepare to meet him. That might mean turning on some worship music, taking this book on a walk, or simply brewing a warm cup of tea or coffee as you settle in.

Hear God's question. "What are you doing here?" (1 Kings 19:9). God isn't asking because he doesn't know. How do you hear the tone of that question? Practice saying it aloud with different intonations: As a mother would say to her son who showed up at her birthday party when he was supposed to be deployed in the military. Like a teenager would say to his mom who showed up, uninvited, to chaperone his prom. Like a mom would say to her toddler while playing peekaboo with a blanket. How does God's voice sound to you? Why do you think that is? God asked Elijah, "What are you doing here, Elijah?" Can you imagine God asking you that same question, with your name, with love in his voice?

Answer God's question. What is your response? Do you know how you are feeling or what you want?

Stay in God's presence. God's presence isn't something we have to conjure up or climb mountaintops to find. Sit in the promise that the Holy Spirit dwells in you; God is with you. Meditate on Psalm 46:10, "Be still, and know that I am God," or 1 Kings 19:9-18. Let yourself be still, put your journal aside, and experience silence.

Listen for the whisper. God doesn't speak on command, and his silence always has a purpose. But when we direct our attention toward him, we allow him to guide our attention and thoughts. What are you noticing? What is distracting you? Is there a different perspective you had not considered? Hold any whisper you hear. Treasure it and test it—God allows us to ask for confirmation and clarification.

Look for goodness. God's love does not always look like fantastic experiences, but his faithfulness never fails. Sometimes we long to see his glory, but he wants to show us his goodness. So whether or not you experienced God's glory, look out for his presence and his goodness around you. Find time to approach him again.

DAY 3   *Read 1 Kings 19:19-21*

The twelve pair of yoked oxen would make readers think of the twelve tribes of Israel, a metaphor for God working with his people. If that number is also literal, it would indicate that Elisha was a successful farmer. Elisha was likely up to his knees in mud and muck when Elijah found him—doing what he was doing, a hard day's work, not knowing that God had already chosen him for an incredible assignment. Throughout the Bible, we see people faithfully working in the simple jobs they've been given: Gideon threshing wheat, Peter fishing, and David out tending sheep. And we learn that not only can that work be preparation for callings we never dreamed we'd have, but God can find us right where we are, however obscure that place may feel.

Have you ever wondered if God was calling you to something? Or wished he would?

Elijah had a coat of camel's hair that was his trademark. As if Steve Jobs handed someone a black turtleneck, when Elijah put his coat on Elisha it was an invitation to grow into it. Elisha was invited to become Elijah's apprentice and wear his prophet's mantle one day.

God provides the gift of a spiritual companion when he sends Elijah, refreshed and restored, back into ministry. Elijah thought he was the only one left, but God had a partner for him who Elijah just hadn't met yet.

Do you have a friend who walks with you, who knows and shares your spiritual journey? How do you find a friend like that? What does it take to be a friend like that?

Elisha asks if he can go home first to say goodbye to his father and mother before joining Elijah. Perhaps you are familiar with the man who was invited to follow Jesus but wanted to go back to say goodbye and bury his father (Luke 9:59), followed by another who asked to first go back and say goodbye to his family (Luke 9:61). Unfortunately, they both unknowingly immortalized themselves in the Bible as people who declined their calling. But that's not what's happening with Elisha.

In the case of the individuals in Luke's Gospel, Bible scholars have noted that it's not clear if the first man's father was sick or even old. He may have been asking to follow Jesus in a different life stage when the patriarch of his family had passed on. That's like saying, "Yes, God. Absolutely. I'll follow you, but my parents would kill me if I didn't finish med school first." Or, "One day, when I'm married, my partner and I will do ministry together." Or, "I'm super busy, but I'll have an empty nest one day. Maybe when I'm retired." That's not following.

But Elijah doesn't see unhealthy procrastination in Elisha's request. Elisha simply wants to say goodbye. More than that, he burns the yoke and cooks the oxen on top, a picture of the sacrifice made by priests and his new calling as a prophet to intercede for God's people. It's also an explicit declaration of not turning back. Elisha isn't keeping farming as a plan B. He's burned his oxen and yoke. He's also feasted and celebrated with his family and town.

There may be times when Jesus calls us, and we drop what we are doing and go. But there may also be times when we say our goodbyes and celebrate what God is doing in us with our community.

Do you see God calling you or someone you know? How can this calling be something that your community supports and celebrates?

REFLECTION: A FAVORITE POEM

Are you feeling spiritually or emotionally stuck in the season or life stage you are in? Are you waiting for something to happen or for someone to find you, longing for a companion to walk alongside you for this next part of your journey? Receive the following Ignatian prayer by Pierre Teilhard de Chardin as a gift.

PATIENT TRUST

Above all, trust in the slow work of God.
We are quite naturally impatient in everything
        to reach the end without delay.
We should like to skip the intermediate stages.
We are impatient of being on the way to
        something unknown, something new.
And yet it is the law of all progress
that it is made by passing through some
        stages of instability—
and that it may take a very
        long time.

And so I think it is with you;
your ideas mature gradually—let them grow,
let them shape themselves, without undue haste.
Don't try to force them on,
as though you could be today what time
(that is to say, grace and circumstances acting
        on your own good will)
will make of you tomorrow.

Only God could say what this new spirit
gradually forming within you will be.
Give Our Lord the benefit
        of believing
that his hand is leading you,
and accept the anxiety of feeling yourself
in suspense and incomplete.

PRAYER: PRAYER PARTNERS

Elijah is at the center of the narrative, but he is not alone. There are prophets in caves nearby, and his assistant is faithfully waiting for God beside him, watching for the miracles of God, praying for the rain and the fire to come. Yet despite reality, Elijah still feels deeply alone. God will remind him that there have always been people who could have carried the burden with him. They could have not only assisted him but companioned him.

Praying with others is intimate. It's vulnerable. You're listening in, advocating for, and sitting with another person before God. You're holding their experiences and entering the story God is writing for them. You're allowing someone else's celebration to shine hope on your desperation and holding back jealousy as the Holy Spirit whispers, "It's okay to want that." Your desires and fears, insecurities, and everything else we intuitively hide become the answer to the question, "How can I pray for you?"

In my loneliest seasons, my prayer partners have created rhythm, connection, and invitations to honesty that I deeply needed.

As you study the Bible and think about creating prayer habits in your life, find your people to pray with. Prayer is an invitation to communion with God and our invitation for God to connect us in community with one another. Prayer is not a strictly private practice.

Here are a few tips I've gathered for making an excellent prayer group.

Set expectations. Are you going to have a one-time prayer group, or meet quarterly or weekly? Set clear boundaries and expectations around the commitment you are making to one another and establish when you will reevaluate how the day, time, and format are working.

Extend the connection. Communicate with one another outside your prayer time. Prayer groups come alongside one another, and prayer times are more meaningful when connections have been cultivated.

Pray. Prayer groups are about talking to God together, but they can quickly turn into talking with one another and virtually leaving God out of the conversation.

Set a limit on request sharing time (this is easier if you've connected over text or in person outside the group) and maximize prayer time.

Learn to say goodbye. Life's rhythms change and many of my prayer groups have evolved and eventually stopped meeting. It's okay when good things have done their work and end, even worth celebrating! What's next? can be a beautiful question.

Ask God who you could invite to pray with you. List a couple of names and reach out to one or two with your idea today. Prayer partners or prayer triads are life changing.

DAY 5

PRACTICE: PAYING ATTENTION

Let's take a few moments from our busy days and our busy minds and pay attention to our present moment. In our study this week, Elijah experiences a breakdown even while he's been close to God. Our pains, desires, hopes, and discouragement can sneak up on us. I tend to overestimate my capacity and ignore the warning signs my body tries to send when I'm overdoing it. *Is anyone else that same way?*

Many thanks to Dave Nixon and Sustainable Faith, who led me through a similar exercise many years ago and helped me to pay attention. Listening to my life has become an essential habit. Use the following figure, Self-Attention, for this exercise.

Let's start with a prayer. Pray Psalm 139:23: "Search me, God, and know my heart; test me and know my anxious thoughts."

Now let's scribble fast. Don't overthink it; write what first pops into your mind.

Take two or three minutes to fill each space.

What is true about your life?

List facts of your life: your relationships, positions, activities, etc. Avoid qualitative words like *kind* or *loving* and focus only on unarguable facts like, "I am a caregiver," "I am single," or "I work fifty hours a week."

SELF-ATTENTION

What is true about your life?

What have you been thinking about?

What emotions have you felt recently?

What is going on with your physical body?

What questions are you holding?

What do you want?

Search me, God, and know my heart;
test me and know my anxious thoughts.

PSALM 139:23

What have you been thinking about?

Note thoughts that come to you regularly, problems you are actively working to solve, something or someone that pops into your mind regularly, a decision you are deliberating, etc. This is different from feelings.

What emotions have you felt recently (including in your dreams)? What triggered them?

These are feelings and emotions, different from thoughts. Things like *sad, lost,* or *betrayed by . . . , ignored by . . . , jealous of . . . , craving . . . , angry at . . . ,* etc.

What is going on with your physical body?

Pause for a moment. Focus on your physical body. Are you feeling tired, sore, weak, or strong? How is your posture? Your libido? Your digestion? Your health?

What question are you holding?

If Jesus were standing in front of you and offered to give you a kind, clear, and honest answer to any question, what would you ask him?

What do you want?

Is there anything you wish you could do, have, be, or feel?

Take two deep breaths in and out. Then, pray Psalm 139:23 again as a prayer, without fear: "Search me, God, and know my heart; test me and know my anxious thoughts."

Read through your answers twice.

- What do you notice?

- Ask God to help you notice what he sees, making meaningful truth stand out from the page and for connections to surface.

- How will you respond?

Remember that you are laying your heart before a gracious, forgiving, loving God who is thrilled to have this conversation with you. Your response to the exercise could range from confession to worship to pursuing a dream or longing you may sense God making clear. It should be motivated by love, not fear or self-improvement. Make an intention to revisit this conversation with him in prayer at any quiet moments you have this week. Be sensitive to notice any presence or response from God.

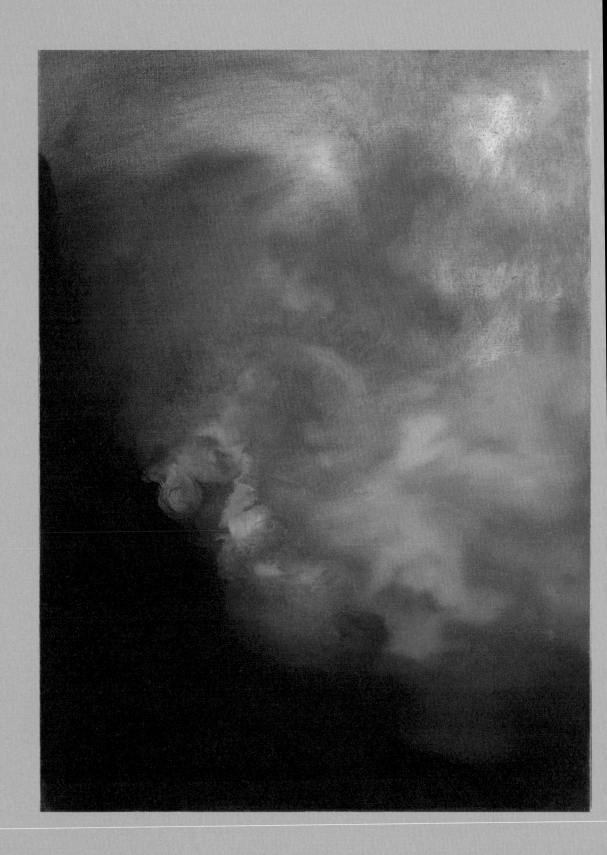

WEEK 5

FORGIVENESS PRAYERS

And forgive us our trespasses,
as we forgive those who
trespass against us.

Why is it so important that you are with God and God alone
on the mountain top? It's important because it's the place in which
you can listen to the voice of the One who calls you the beloved.
To pray is to listen to the One who calls you my beloved daughter,
my beloved son, my beloved child. To pray is to let that voice
speak to the center of your being, to your guts, and
let that voice resound in your whole being.

HENRI NOUWEN

GROUP SESSION

Being forgiven is a life-transforming result of prayers for mercy. Forgiveness brings freedom from guilt, shame, and fear. Being forgiven makes us a forgiver of others.

SUMMARY OF WEEK FOUR

- Elijah experienced burnout, and God met him right where he was.
- Elijah moved toward God, and God met him in an unexpected way.
- Elijah was alone, and God gave him community.

What stood out to you last week? Was there something from your study, your life, or your conversations with God that you would like to share?

VIEW THE WEEK FIVE VIDEO

Notes

- Forgiveness is freedom. Receive it.

- Forgiveness is freedom. Share it.

- Forgiveness is freedom. Live in it.

- Forgiveness is freedom. Let it heal you.

  - Sin done *to you* will injure you.
  - Sin done *by you* can trap you in shame.
  - And sin done *around you* can wrap you in fear.

- Forgiveness is freedom. Enjoy it.

DISCUSS

1. How often do you forgive or receive forgiveness in your daily life?

2. What is the most helpful thing you have heard about forgiveness?

3. What is the least helpful thing you have heard about forgiveness?

4. How have your experiences of being forgiven or unforgiven affected how you think about forgiveness?

5. If there's someone you are struggling to forgive, what makes that complicated for you?

ALL TOGETHER: LECTIO DIVINA

As we reflect on how God answers prayers for forgiveness, let's think of how we ask for forgiveness or expect God to respond.

I wrote in my first book, *God's Many Voices: Learning to Listen, Expectant to Hear,*

Throughout church history, Catholics, Protestants, and Puritans have used a similar approach to read the Bible deeply in conversation with God. It has been called divine reading, lectio divina, or spiritual reading. Honoring the overlap and commonality of these, we can call it contemplative reading, a process that looks something like this:

Prepare yourself to read.

Read the Scripture slowly, multiple times.

Let the Holy Spirit draw your attention to a word or phrase.

Pray about what you have read, connecting personally.

Leave space to listen for God's response.

We're going to read of a person who the religious leaders didn't think was worthy to touch the feet of Jesus, let alone be forgiven by God. Listen for the elements of forgiveness and also love.

To begin, let's prepare ourselves to read. This might look like a moment of silence or some deep breathing. I like to light a candle and play soft instrumental music to make a space of calm focus.

Ask someone to read Luke 7:36-48, slowly and with expression, twice.

Leave two minutes of silence. Ask the Holy Spirit to draw your attention to a word, image, or idea in the passage.

Ask someone to read Luke 7:36-48, slowly, one more time.

Pray about what you have read. Take whatever has drawn your attention, sparked your emotion, or raised a question to God in prayer.

Leave one minute of silence to listen for God's response.

Let the timekeeper end with an "amen."

Take time to reflect. What did you take away from that experience?

PRAYING TOGETHER: CONFESSION

You are invited to communal confession, but you may choose not to participate or not to participate aloud. There are three parts: meditation, prayer, and welcome.

Meditation. Take time to read the following verses about God's forgiveness and meditate on what a God who forgives in this way is like.

Psalm 32:1-5

Matthew 18:21-35

1 John 1:9

Prayer. Pray together to receive God's forgiveness and invitation to move forward free of guilt, shame, or hypocrisy. *You can choose to pray silently or aloud.* If you feel safe, you are encouraged to pray aloud to be fully seen and fully forgiven. Have one person lead the prayer by introducing the following sections or assign different people to begin each prompt when the time is right.

1. God, we need your forgiveness for what we have done and have not done (for our families, our friends, our neighbors, and others). Help us restore these relationships.

2. God, we need your forgiveness for the ways we have hardened our hearts to the needs or stories of others. Make our hearts tender to others and help us to not look away.

3. God, we need your forgiveness for the unforgiveness we carry, even though you have forgiven us. Help us to forgive.

4. God, we need forgiveness for the things that keep us from being closer to you. Help us to love you more.

5. God, thank you for your promise to forgive. Help us to receive your forgiveness with awareness of our freedom and your love.

6. Amen.

Welcome. Breathe deeply in and out. That may have been a level of trust that was new for some.

We have all admitted we were wrong, said we are sorry, and been forgiven.

Turn to the person beside you and say, "You are forgiven, and I am forgiven, and I'm so glad to be here and human with you," or "We are forgiven, and we are loved just as we are."

SOLO STUDY

Some easy adjustments if you are on this journey with us, but without a group:

- Read the lectio divina aloud to yourself. It does make a difference for your ears to hear the words, so read it audibly or play the passage from an audio Bible. Follow the rest of the activity on your own.

- Read the verses for meditation and do your own prayers, but find a safe person to share your experience with at whatever level of detail you feel comfortable. Receive the acceptance in their eyes and the assurance from a brother or sister that God has forgiven you just as he said he would.

DAY 1   *Read 1 Kings 21:1-29*

We don't have to wait for the prophet to tell us that what Ahab did was wrong this time. How many injustices or evil actions can you name from this passage?

Ahab wanted something and didn't get it. Jezebel convinced him that he *deserved* it. She knew they had the power to manipulate the circumstances and make it happen. They didn't need to be given the land, they could take it, and the cost didn't matter. They could corrupt a city government, hijack a religious holiday, murder an innocent man—robbing his family of him as well as his land—and have the blood of Naboth not only on them but on the men they bribed and deceived.

If anything should shock us about this episode, it is not how evil the queen and king were (that was well known); the truly shocking thing is that God received Ahab's repentance and temporarily relented in his judgment. After all that Ahab had done, when he showed humility by publicly expressing his despair over his sin by wearing rough, shoddy clothes and covering himself with ashes, God showed mercy. The prophesied end of Ahab would still come (1 Kings 21:19, 28) but his repentance was met with mercy and a stay of judgment—if only that posture of humble repentance had characterized the rest of his life, what might have happened?

I was a volunteer prison chaplain for a few years, and more than one woman told me that I could never understand her life. She'd hint that I had no idea what she had done and that I wouldn't be talking to her if I knew. No one in her family or on a jury would ever forgive her—God would never forgive her, either.

I wondered who told her about God, as though he were the harshest judge in the system.

I wonder who has told *you* about God. What did they tell you would happen if you did something wrong?

What do you think God would do if you broke six out of ten commandments on one day, and one of them was murder? But that is what Ahab did! We know precisely how God would respond to genuine repentance; we watch with jaws on the floor as he does it.

And we wonder, *Is there anything I can do that God couldn't forgive?*

> The most scandalous thing about God isn't his anger, it's his forgiveness.

The most scandalous thing about God isn't his anger, it's his forgiveness. There's another story about another prophet, Jonah (yep, swallowed-by-a-fish Jonah), who God sent to Ninevah, the most evil, violent, notorious town of his time. Jonah met that fish because he originally ran away from God and his mission. Why? Because Jonah would have happily watched that town burn to the ground. He wanted God's judgment to come, not his forgiveness. The people of Ninevah also unexpectedly repent and temporarily turn to God, delaying their ultimate end. As Jonah expresses his frustration with God over the mercy that was extended to the evil city, Jonah repeats a truth we find several times over in the Old Testament: "I knew that you are a gracious and compassionate God, slow to anger and abounding in love, a God who relents from sending calamity" (Jonah 4:2). Do you recognize that from Week 1, Day 1?

God confronts evil and makes space for peace, goodness, creation, and growth in its place. . . . God's judgment is a good thing.

Jesus ultimately confronted evil on the cross, and through his resurrection, we're invited to live in the freedom of being forgiven. We make mistakes, and our inner shadows show, but the most dangerous thing we can do is forget that God wants to forgive us. God is sitting on the front porch, waiting for our hearts to break, our humility to take hold, our fear to be set aside so that we can approach him at our worst, trusting he has the power and the compassion to forgive us—because his love has never given up on us.

How do you feel about God's forgiveness being available to even the worst people?

Do you ever feel internal resistance about asking God for forgiveness? Why?

REFLECTION: THE JOY OF CONFESSION

When (not if) we make mistakes, the metaphor we have for God matters.

Is God our Father who we try to hide our mistakes from so we don't get in trouble?

Is God a judge we come to begging for mercy and a clear record?

Is God far away and probably didn't notice or doesn't care, so why bring it up?

Remember the image you chose of God in Week 1? Does that image you hold change when you feel guilt or shame?

What if we imagined God waiting to forgive us instead of waiting to punish us?

God knows how destructive sin is. Confession is our agreement with God. Sin isn't something fun God is keeping us from; it has the power to destroy relationships, hurt innocent people, and shape our thoughts in unhealthy ways. God is offering to save us.

Psalm 32 says that when we confess our sin, it is forgiven, covered, and not counted. When we agree with God that what we have done is wrong and harmful to us and others, and we want to choose a different way—God's way—next time, that is confession and repentance. God does not always clear all the consequences and effects of our choice, but our dangerous choice is forgiven and cleansed. Not only that, but God will not hold it in our face later; it is covered, hidden by God instead of by me. It is not even counted. God doesn't track how many times he has forgiven your sin. He won't start the conversation with, "How am I supposed to take you seriously when you keep messing up the same way?" So don't be afraid to confess something for the hundredth time.

Those sins that we keep confessing aren't proof that we don't deserve forgiveness. They prove that we keep agreeing with God no matter how much we struggle. God may ask us to forgive the same person seventy-seven times or seventy times seven—either way, the number seven's representation of perfection essentially makes it imperative to forgive one another infinitely (Matthew 18:22). That's not because God sets impossible standards—it's a beautiful picture of the way he forgives us. There is no end to his mercy, which should always be sufficient fuel for us to extend mercy to others.

DAY 2 — Read Luke 15:11-32

Have you ever said or done something and realized you went too far—that bridge was burned, and there are no second chances? This story was told in a way to make it clear that this young man burned the bridge and then set the box of matches on fire.

I want to read it as an apology, forgiveness, and reconciliation story. When I do, my stomach sinks, and I think of how hard it is to say sorry. Something about admitting I made a mistake makes me feel instantly unworthy of love, connection, or reliance. I brace myself for the worst, and like the younger son, I resign myself to being unloved, untrusted, and unwelcome. I think that might be one reason why Jesus doesn't tell this story as a story of "sorry" and "I forgive you." Instead, he talks about the son's return in a set of three stories about how we celebrate when something we lost is found.

Imagine having a child who threw a massive fit in a mall, threw their middle finger up at you, and walked away. When you gathered yourself together, you started looking for them, but they were nowhere to be found. A few hours later, mall security had retrieved their phone from a bathroom trashcan. You drove home without them in your car and waited while the police did their best. What would you do the first moment your child emerged through the flashing lights from the squad cars out front, wrapped in a blanket? I would run to my baby and wrap my arms around them as fast and tight as possible— the rest of the consequences and lecture could wait. I thought my most precious person was lost, but they've been found. That's how Jesus says God receives us when we come home—running to embrace us, love us, welcome us, even trust us (could you believe that signet ring?), because no matter what needs to be worked out, we were lost, and now we are home, and we were always God's precious child.

When I come home to God, I think of returning to my own house and parents after doing something wrong. There was not a lot of warm welcome in those memories. They once threatened to turn me in to the police when I was seven, and made me pack a grocery bag with what I wanted to take to jail. They thought they were teaching me a positive lesson, but the one I learned was really Do. Not. Get. Caught. Lock that secret up tight and never tell anybody about it. And if you do get caught . . . well . . .

How did you deal with getting caught doing something wrong as a kid? How did the authority figures in your life respond when you made mistakes?

How do you think your ideas of family and home shape your ideas about forgiveness or confession?

Remember from Week 1 that the image we have for who God is and what he is like radically affects how we pray—especially when we feel lost, unworthy, and far from home.

In what ways can you recognize the God who Moses knew from Exodus 34:5-7 in the story of the lost son?

> Then the LORD came down in the cloud and stood there with him and proclaimed his name, the LORD. And he passed in front of Moses, proclaiming, "The LORD, the LORD, the *compassionate and gracious* God, *slow to anger, abounding in love and faithfulness*, maintaining love to thousands, and *forgiving wickedness, rebellion and sin*. Yet he *does not leave the guilty unpunished*; he punishes the children and their children for the sin of the parents to the third and fourth generation." (emphasis added)

REFLECTION: WRITTEN PRAYER

The lost son rehearsed his apology on the road home. He planned what he would say to his father. If you want to "come home," either with an apology or like the older son, simply come out of the fringes of the estate and spend more time with your Father in the main house—eat breakfast at the counter and be comfortable in your jammies in the kitchen—like you really belong in the family. What could you say to God?

Take the time to write it out. Tell him how you feel. Ask him if you are welcomed, loved, trusted. Read it aloud when you are finished. Listen for his answer today and in the days to come.

> The LORD your God is with you,
>> the Mighty Warrior who saves.
> He will take great delight in you;
>> in his love he will no longer rebuke you,
>> but will rejoice over you with singing. (Zephaniah 3:17)

If this story captured your imagination, you will enjoy one of my favorite books—*The Return of the Prodigal Son: A Story of Homecoming* by Henri Nouwen. Add it to your wish list or nightstand; you won't regret it.

Love prospers when a fault is forgiven,
but dwelling on it separates close friends.

PROVERBS 17:9 NLT

Forgiveness, then, is a form of voluntary suffering. In forgiving,
rather than retaliating, you make a choice to bear the cost.

TIMOTHY KELLER

Forgiveness isn't just between us and God; we pray that God would help us to forgive others as he has forgiven us. Forgiving others is hard. Sometimes they aren't sorry. Sometimes they aren't alive. Sometimes we wish they weren't alive—there is no way we can imagine being in a close relationship with them that feels safe ever again.

My favorite book on forgiveness is *The Book of Forgiving: The Fourfold Path for Healing Ourselves and Our World* by Desmond Tutu and his daughter Mpho Tutu. Desmond Tutu was the chairman of the Truth and Reconciliation Commission in South Africa, which attempted to apply restorative justice in the wake of apartheid—government-sanctioned racial segregation leading to some of the most heinous crimes ever committed. He identified the four-step process of forgiveness—telling the story, naming the hurt, granting forgiveness, and renewing or releasing the relationship. It was the first time I had seen the process so clearly, and I also recognized that forgiveness does not always mean restoring the relationship. I can release the offender along with the offense.

It has helped me tremendously to understand forgiveness in terms of debt. Someone owed me something and now hasn't paid me. Whether it was a friend who owed me confidentiality or a mother who owed me care, there was an expectation or agreement that has left me poorer and bearing the cost of them not holding up their end of the deal. I have some choices:

1. I can be a victim who worries over the cost of a bill they do not intend to pay.

2. I can be bitter that I am suffering because they failed to give me what they should have.

3. I can negotiate the bill with them because I don't want it to come between us.

4. I can absorb the cost of the bill because I know they cannot or will not pay.

I've held many unpaid bills in my hand. Some I want to resolve, but some I send to collections (God will judge everything in the end) and don't expect to ever see a cent. I may be poorer for having been owed, but I have seen the cost of unforgiveness in too many people who become bitter, helpless, or cynical. God's invitation to forgiveness isn't a call for martyrs to give up on what they are owed; it's the road to freedom for people who refuse to be made victims twice—once by the debt and then by their own unforgiveness.

Do you know anyone who lives under the crushing weight of unforgiveness?

Is there a debt you need to settle before it crushes you?

REFLECTION: SETTLING THE BILL

Is there someone who comes to mind who didn't give you what you deserved or took something from you and owes you for the ways they have cost you?

GUEST CHECK

| DATE | SERVER | TABLE | QUESTS | CHECK NUMBER |
| | | | | 689561 |

TAX

TOTAL

Thank You - Please Come Again

Set a timer for five minutes and write what happened between you. Then make a bullet list of at least three things they failed to do or specific ways they hurt you. Write up a bill for what you think they owe you. Decide whether it is worth your time, energy, and focus to settle the tab with them and find a way to restore your relationship. If so, remember the incredible mercy God has shown you, and pray that he will be with you as you humbly bring the issues to their attention. If not, grieve the loss that you've experienced. Write *unpaid* on the bill and release it to God. Ask him in prayer to bring justice to the situation in a way that only he can. Release what you are owed to him. Ask him to provide what you need, even as you keenly feel what you lack. Ask him to free you from the victimhood or bitterness of being owed. Do not let your debtor take anything else from your future.

DAY 4

PRAYER: PRAYING SCRIPTURE

When you don't have the words to pray, pray God's words. Let them guide your prayers. Emphasize different words as you pray the verse, and let each word guide your prayers deeper.

Try praying Luke 6:37 (emphasis added):

Do not *judge*, and you will not be *judged*. Do not condemn, and you will not be condemned. Forgive, and you will be forgiven.

Is there someone I am judging right now? Do I know their motives and their story? Am I the one who God has appointed to judge them? Am I being judged? Does this truth free me from shame?

Do not *judge*, and you will not be *judged*. Do not condemn, and you will not be condemned. Forgive, and you will be forgiven.

Is there someone who I have given up on or punished instead of forgiving? Is there someone who has given up on me? How can God's forgiveness enter that situation?

Do not **judge**, and you will not be **judged**. Do not condemn, and you will not be condemned. Forgive, and you will be forgiven.

How have I been forgiven? Are there more places in my life forgiveness can heal? Where am I withholding forgiveness from others? What kind of forgiveness does that situation call for (release or restoration)?

Other verses that work well for prayer (emphasis added):

I *sought* the Lord, and he *answered* me;
    he *delivered* me from all my *fears*. (Psalm 34:4)

Instead, *be kind* to each other, tenderhearted, *forgiving* one another, *just as God* through Christ has forgiven you. (Ephesians 4:32 NLT)

If we are *unfaithful*,

    he remains *faithful*,

    for he cannot deny *who he is*. (2 Timothy 2:13 NLT)

For you know that when your faith is *tested*, your *endurance* has a chance to *grow*. (James 1:3 NLT)

Give all your *worries and cares* to God, for he *cares* about you. (1 Peter 5:7 NLT)

DAY 5

All the things in this world are gifts of God, created for us, to be the means by which we can come to know him better, love him more surely, and serve him more faithfully. As a result, we ought to appreciate and use these gifts of God insofar as they help us toward our goal of loving service and union with God. But insofar as any created things hinder our progress toward our goal, we ought to let them go.

SAINT IGNATIUS OF LOYOLA

PRACTICE: GRATITUDE JOURNALING

As we pray to be open to forgive and be forgiven, we remember the story Jesus told of an ungrateful servant in Matthew 18:21-35. That servant had a huge debt forgiven and was offered the freedom of a fresh start. Instead of being grateful or offering mercy to someone who owed him, he demanded what he was owed.

Being ready to forgive is a result of realizing how forgiven we are, that we are shaping our lives into the family resemblance of a God who forgives, and abandoning our entitlement to celebrate how many gifts in our lives we don't deserve. Take the time to notice God's presence, beauty, and gifts that fill the world we live in. Let's pray some prayers of gratitude and praise for the way God has already moved in the sunrise today, through the friend who offered to help, or in how far you have come from the earlier chapters in your story.

Choose at least two gratitude practices to increase your attention to God today.

Gratitude lists. Quickly jot lists (usually only a few words per line) of things and people you are thankful for. Consider keeping a journal. There are lots of options—a paper journal, a note in your calendar, a running chalkboard list, or an app for your phone. Here are some ideas to get your pen moving:

1. People who have given you a chance
2. Things that delight your five senses
3. Things that make you laugh
4. Things that draw your attention to detail or beauty
5. Things in your home that you use or appreciate often
6. People who add to your life
7. Words that meant something to you
8. Things that make you think of love
9. Ways you are able to relax or unwind
10. Ways you are able to be creative or productive
11. Unexpected surprises

Responsive writing. Set a timer and write for five minutes about one thing or person you are grateful for. Maybe it was a second chance you were offered. Keep your pen moving without overthinking what you are writing or trying to make it perfect. Share what you've written with someone else, read it aloud, or post it online. You may be surprised at how the way you've experienced goodness connects with and inspires the people around you.

Gratitude walk. Take a walk and be purposeful about noticing good things and the marks of good people having done good work all around you. It doesn't have to be a gorgeous nature hike; it could even be around your house. Consider keeping a bullet journal or snapping pictures on your phone to document the things you find that spark gratitude.

Remembrance. Gratitude is so sweet in the moment, and then so easy to forget. How will you remember the things you are grateful for? One idea could be to start an album on your phone titled "gratitude" that you can store snapshots in and scroll through later. What do you think will work best for you to keep track of God's good gifts?

Move it forward. So many of the gifts that we enjoy were made possible by God through other people. What can you say or do or give to someone today to add to the beauty and goodness in their world? Is there an opportunity for you to show someone mercy or forgiveness?

Prayer. The best sort of gratitude is when all the grace that surrounds us brings us closer to God, the center of joy. Take some time to thank God for who he is and the beauty he has surrounded you with—not only for the things he has given and the ways we enjoy them but also for who he is as a generous giver who sees us and knows us.

PRAYERS OF
THE DELIVERED

And lead us not into temptation,
but deliver us from evil.

We must lay before him what is in us; not what ought to be in us.

C. S. LEWIS

GROUP SESSION

We are tempted in countless ways to choose any other way but God's. We'll see one king of Israel fail and then watch the future King Jesus resist temptation, leaving a path for us to choose God's way too.

SUMMARY OF WEEK FIVE

- The most scandalous thing about God isn't his anger, it's his forgiveness.
- Apologizing is homecoming.
- Forgiveness is freedom.

What stood out to you last week? Was there something from your study, your life, or your conversations with God that you would like to share?

Notes

- The end of Elijah's life is a radical homecoming.

- The end of Elijah's life is a handoff.

- The end of Elijah's life is the beginning of his legacy.

- The end of Elijah's life couldn't be seen in the middle.

- Your middle is not your end.

DISCUSS

1. What do you want your legacy to be?

2. What does it feel like to be in the middle of your own story right now?

3. How has studying Elijah's journey over the past five weeks affected the way you talk to God?

ALL TOGETHER—PRAYING TOGETHER: PRAYER POWER HOUR

In celebration of this journey we've shared, we are going to pray. I remember the first time our group attempted to pray for an hour. Our usual routine was to spend twenty minutes sharing our updates and prayer requests, and then someone would pray for around five minutes to summarize all of those because we were always running out of time. Praying as a group for sixty minutes felt like a stretch. It was. Somehow, though, the power hour format made it easy, and the time flew by. Everyone wanted to keep going after the time was up. People felt focused, empowered, and we experienced the peace and joy that come uniquely from being in the presence of God with one another.

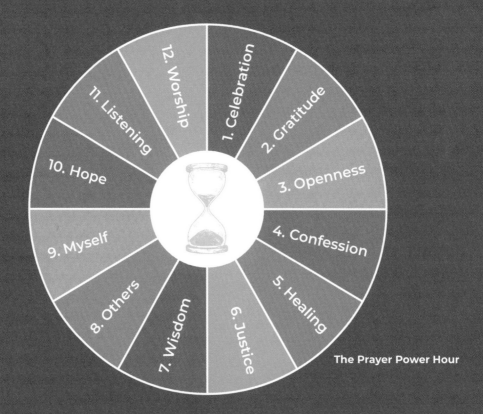

The Prayer Power Hour

0:00 — CELEBRATION.

Thank God for who he is. "Thank you, God, that you are . . ."

For great is your love, reaching to the heavens;
your faithfulness reaches to the skies. (Psalm 57:10)

0:05 — GRATITUDE.

Thank God as the giver of the good gifts in your life.

Every good and perfect gift is from above, coming down from the Father of the
heavenly lights, who does not change like shifting shadows. (James 1:17)

0:10 — OPENNESS.

Come to God with a desire to speak and to listen, to connect in prayer.

Search me, God, and know my heart; test me and know my anxious thoughts.
(Psalm 139:23)

0:15 — CONFESSION.

Release the tension of anything that has come between you and God.

If we confess our sins, he is faithful and just and will forgive us our sins and purify us
from all unrighteousness. (1 John 1:9)

0:20 — PRAYERS FOR HEALING.

After you have received your forgiveness through confession, bring the needs of anyone
who needs spiritual or physical healing before God.

Therefore confess your sins to each other and pray for each other so that you may
be healed. The prayer of a righteous person is powerful and effective. (James 5:16)

0:25 — PRAYERS FOR JUSTICE.

Pray for God's good definition of justice to be made known and made reality in issues that face your community, culture, and world.

> *He has shown you, O mortal, what is good.*
> *And what does the LORD require of you?*
> *To act justly and to love mercy*
> *and to walk humbly with your God. (Micah 6:8)*

0:30 — PRAYERS FOR WISDOM.

For yourself, people you know, or public figures who have important decisions coming up or who are wrestling through God's best vision for the future.

> *Whether you turn to the right or to the left, your ears will hear a voice behind you, saying, "This is the way; walk in it." (Isaiah 30:21)*

0:35 — PRAYERS FOR OTHERS.

For anyone you know with any need.

> *Elijah was a human being, even as we are. He prayed earnestly that it would not rain, and it did not rain on the land for three and a half years. (James 5:17)*

0:40 — PRAYERS FOR MYSELF.

For any need you have.

> *Ask and it will be given to you; seek and you will find; knock and the door will be opened to you. For everyone who asks receives; the one who seeks finds; and to the one who knocks, the door will be opened. (Matthew 7:7-8)*

0:45 — PRAYERS FOR HOPE.

To surrender these wants, needs, and hurts into the hands of a kind and good God, and to trust that he has heard and will respond.

> *Immediately the boy's father exclaimed, "I do believe; help me overcome my unbelief!" (Mark 9:24)*

0:50 — SILENT LISTENING.

Leave space in silent prayer for God to respond to you or make his presence known.

> *After the earthquake came a fire, but the LORD was not in the fire. And after the fire came a gentle whisper. When Elijah heard it, he pulled his cloak over his face and went out and stood at the mouth of the cave.*
>
> > *Then a voice said to him, "What are you doing here, Elijah?"*
> > *(1 Kings 19:13)*

0:55 — WORSHIP.

Celebrate what God has done in the past to show himself good, and entrust the future to him.

> *I have always been mindful of your unfailing love*
> *and have lived in reliance on your faithfulness. (Psalm 26:3)*

1:00 — AMEN.

The prayer power hour was inspired by *The Hour That Changes the World: A Practical Plan for Personal Prayer*, a brilliant book by Dick Eastman.

Here's how the prayer power hour works:

1. You do not need to take prayer requests ahead of time; we will all be joining one another as we pray for what we want to talk to God about.

2. There are twelve time increments of three to five minutes each. Each increment has a theme.

3. One person manages the time, and as close to the right minute as possible, they introduce the next theme and read the verse. You can also have the time manager point to a delegate for the different sections so that different people can introduce each section, but only one person watches the clock.

4. After each prayer section has been introduced, the group prays. Some may pray silently, but many pray aloud.

5. Since there are only five minutes in each section (a little less since there was an introduction), everyone can keep their prayers short.

6. As you pray, pray to God, not to the group. Allow them to listen in but keep your prayers and attention directed to God.

7. As others are praying, listen to them and join them in bringing their words to God. Resist the temptation to rehearse what you plan to say next.

8. Not everyone will pray in every section; you may pray whenever there is something you want to talk to God about.

9. Our group enjoyed having instrumental music playing quietly in the background, but that is optional.

SOLO STUDY

An easy adjustment if you are on this journey with us, but without a group:

- Try the power prayer hour (or pray for thirty-six minutes using three-minute intervals) on your own. It may feel like a stretch initially, but you might surprise yourself at the way time flies!

DAY 1 — *Read 2 Kings 1:1-18*

King Ahaziah follows King Ahab, both on the throne and in his worship of Baal. When he is injured to the brink of death, who does he turn to? He sends messengers to Ekron, more than forty miles away, to consult an oracle that would seek a spiritual connection with Baal-zebub or one of his servants. Sorcery, communication with evil spirits, and homage to gods other than the true God of Israel were absolutely forbidden. When Ahaziah asks if he is going to recover, he is likely also asking how he might recover. He is asking the oracle of Baal if he will live and what he must do to ensure that. In Matthew 10:25, Jesus uses the name Beelzebul, the equivalent of Baal-zebub, to refer to the devil himself.

In modern terms, the king of Israel is sending messengers to make a deal with the devil for his life.

It is less interesting to reflect on how outrageously wrong that is than to ask, Why was Ahaziah consulting Baal when God had already demonstrated on Mount Carmel that Baal was powerless? Why not go to God with his problem?

Maybe God played such a small part in Ahaziah's daily life that when he went to solve the problem of his injury, God didn't come to mind.

Maybe he had consulted the prophets of God before, but he didn't like what they had to say and had gotten in the habit of ignoring them.

Maybe someone in his court said, "Hey, I know someone . . ." and even though it was against every law, tradition, and word of wisdom he knew, he was intrigued.

Maybe in his reign so far he had lost control of Moab, filled the palace with pagan idols, enjoyed the feasts and sexual rituals of Baal worship, and avoided talking to God. But on the other hand, maybe his leadership insecurity or the fact he didn't want to give up the pleasure he had surrounded himself with was what kept him from the prophets.

We don't know for sure what was in the mind of Ahaziah, but I know those are some things that keep me from praying about things in my life. Before we skip ahead and begin to judge, take a moment and remember the last few times that you've encountered trouble—an injury, illness, an accident, a loss. *Where did you go first?*

What is it that sends you to a search engine, a podcast, an influencer, a horoscope, or elsewhere instead of prayer? Does God feel too far away or too slow? Are you afraid you would have to take his advice in areas of your life where you don't want to listen to him? Or is prayer just not something you even think of?

The king was so mad when his messengers were interrupted by Elijah that he sent his military to go and kill him. Elijah calls fire from heaven again. As he sits alone and vulnerable, Elijah calls on God for his protection. God responds to Elijah's prayer for fire again. He saves Elijah's life and sends another clear message to the king that he is God and Baal is not.

Is there an important area of your life that you haven't been talking to God about?

REFLECTION: STAINED GLASS PRAYER

A few years ago, I had the incredible privilege of visiting the Sainte-Chapelle in Paris. Long ago, people who didn't own Bibles connected to God through the stained glass windows they visited in cathedrals. Some of these glass panels told stories, and others displayed the transcendent beauty of light filtered through burned sand. While standing in that Parisian chapel, craning my neck upward, those awe-inspiring windows brought me so close to God's beauty that they filled me with a desire for his light. The rose window outlined here stopped me in my tracks and invited me to pray.

We're going to pray with and through art. You don't have to like art to connect with God this way. Something about the tactile nature of putting pen to paper, the visual stimulation of colors on a page, and the slow pace of taking our time before moving on make stained glass prayers a worthwhile exercise for everyone to try.

We've seen Ahaziah's example of how easy it is to forget to consult God for wisdom, so today our prayer is going to focus on inviting God's wisdom, correction, goodness, and hope into different areas of our lives.

Find some colorful pencils, pens, or markers, and let this stained glass window pattern be a guide for your prayer. Use as many colors as you like for each expanding ring.

Sainte-Chapelle rose window

1. Think of a name for God as you pray. Is it healer? Shepherd? Friend? Provider? Color the center encircled rosette with color(s) that remind you of God and his nature as you approach him in prayer.

2. As you color the leafy ring just outside the center circle, consult God for wisdom in any relationships that are on your mind. Use colors that might reflect these.

3. As you color the next ring that looks a bit like raindrops filled with oak leaves, consult God for wisdom in any career or financial goals that you have. Use colors that might reflect these.

4. As you color the thin outer ring that includes shapes like hearts, consult God for wisdom concerning your own physical, spiritual, and mental health. Use colors that might reflect these.

5. As you color in the final frame and corners of the window that contains all your prayers, thank God for his attention. Commit to continue to listen for his voice in these areas. His answer to your request could be coming through people, circumstances, or other ways in the coming weeks.

DAY 2
Read Matthew 4:1-11; Hebrews 4:14-16; 1 Corinthians 10:12-13; James 1:15

Jesus lived a human life. It's easy to get caught up in the perfection of his morality and forget that his life was far from easy. Long before the cross, he faced loneliness, insults, pain, disappointment, grief, and even temptation. Jesus' temptation story reminds me of Elijah and Moses again—wandering for forty days, coming from an intense high point with God (his baptism and anointing) to a painful low point right after. But Jesus doesn't encounter God on a mountain—he's faced with Satan in the wilderness.

When Satan tempted Jesus to turn the stone into bread, what do you think Satan would have accomplished if Jesus had given in?

When Satan tempted Jesus to jump from the highest point of the temple, what do you think Satan would have accomplished if Jesus had given in?

When Satan tempted Jesus to worship him, what do you think Satan would have accomplished if Jesus had given in?

The wilderness temptation is a passage you can return to again and again. (You might even try it as a lectio divina.)

Jesus was fully loyal to God and surrendered to God's authority and wisdom for what was good, beautiful, and true. Adam and Eve couldn't resist Satan's temptation to be their own source of wisdom for living their life apart from dependence on God. Many days I entertain the temptation to make my own plan or rely on my own ideas. Jesus shows it's possible to resist even Satan himself—and later the apostle Paul would promise that there is always a way out of temptation. It might be awkward, but you can always get away.

> When Jesus emptied himself of his privilege and power as God and put on human flesh, he stepped into the full human experience.

Some people see Jesus' temptation as theater. He was God's perfect Son; he would always be sinless, but here was his chance to prove it. The thing is, the Holy Spirit led Jesus into the wilderness *to be tempted*. The writer of Hebrews tells us that Jesus knows what it is like to be "tempted in every way, *just as we are*" (Hebrews 4:15, emphasis added). He knows what it's like to be hungry, to want to take a shortcut, to want to avoid pain. When Jesus emptied himself of his privilege and power as God and put on human flesh, he stepped into the full human experience.

Temptation can come from many places—willpower is rarely enough to get out of it. Pray for wisdom. As you pray the Lord's Prayer, consider also memorizing 1 Corinthians 10:13 and plan some escape routes from common temptations. As you plan ahead, remember how much it can help when your hormones or dopamine levels are balanced with diet, exercise, rest, medication, or other means to help you resist some of the temptations you feel like you can't shake. Remember that your body and spirit are connected. Spiritual enemies may deceive, attack, or tempt you, but you don't have to face your demons in a desert alone. Jesus understands how torn we feel, and you have people nearby who love you enough to pray with you through anything—don't be afraid to reach out to them.

What temptation to choose your way instead of God's way are you struggling with?

How can believing that Jesus knows how hard it is to resist temptation change how you pray?

REFLECTION: WANT TO WANT TO

Immediately the boy's father exclaimed, "I do believe; help me overcome my unbelief!" (Mark 9:24)

These are perhaps the most relatable words in Scripture. When it comes to temptation, I want to want to escape it. I have a tough time praying to ask God for help because sometimes I don't want help. I'd rather not talk about it with God. I'm not ready to give it up. It's good to get curious about why some things are so hard to let go of—what they're giving us and what they're taking away. If you're not ready to repent, think about praying the "Want to want to" prayer: "I want to live in freedom, unashamed and joyful in the presence of God; God help me overcome my competing desires."

This honest prayer begins a conversation with God that may be ongoing for longer than you like. The inner battle has been waged aggressively for all the followers of Jesus—even the most respected, like Paul:

> So I find this law at work: Although I want to do good, evil is right there with me. For in my inner being I delight in God's law; but I see another law at work in me, waging war against the law of my mind and making me a prisoner of the law of sin at work within me. What a wretched man I am! Who will rescue me from this body that is subject to death? Thanks be to God, who delivers me through Jesus Christ our Lord! (Romans 7:21-25)

The point is not to purge ourselves of sin so we can be better than everyone else—or good enough for God. At their best, our temptations can make us more dependent on God (2 Corinthians 12:7-9). If we avoid confession, we might find ourselves avoiding prayer. Instead, we can take even our own unrepentance, our own desperate clinging to comfort or pleasure or the good opinion of others, and even that can become an open-hearted prayer.

Pray with me if you want to want to as much as I do. *"I want to live in freedom, unashamed and joyful in the presence of God; God help me overcome my competing desires."*

DAY 3   *Read James 1:15; Psalm 86:5; Galatians 5:1*

Deliverance from temptation can come through confession. It rarely comes without it, or without the witness of others—as much as we naturally want to hide.

My spiritual director traced an invisible cross on my forehead, looked me in the eye with warmth and kindness, and recited 1 John 1:9: "If we confess our sins, he is faithful and just and will forgive us our sins and purify us from all unrighteousness."

I had been carrying the weight of a secret that was beginning to sit sour in my stomach. I had confessed it too many times to God; now I was embarrassed to admit to him that I still didn't feel better, still didn't feel changed, or even forgiven. I asked my spiritual director if she would receive my confession. It wasn't our regular practice, but she obliged. Then, as the embodied presence I needed, she reminded me that God had forgiven me.

Almost a decade later, I still see the acceptance and love in her eyes when I ask God for forgiveness. I think it had been too hard for me to imagine his compassion, welcome, and understanding before I had seen it on a human face. Other times when I've asked people in my life for forgiveness, I've sensed obligation, reluctance, or disappointment. I think those were the faces I was imagining God wearing. I hadn't learned how to accept God's type of forgiveness—the kind of forgiveness we discussed in the Week 5 Group Session or Week 5, Day 1 Reflection.

Confession, saying out loud what we want to be forgiven for, has always been individual *and* communal in the church (James 5:16). It is our chance to show one another the face of God, to remind each other that we are utterly and completely forgiven. All we need to do is lay down our pride, admit we were wrong, say we are sorry, and ask for forgiveness. When Jesus died on the cross, the forgiveness that made it possible for us to be in God's family was extended. When we receive that forgiveness, it's ours. As we live our lives, we might be free from the power of sin, but we are still tempted, we give in, we make mistakes. Confessing these sins as they happen is important because even though they don't change our relationship as children of God, when we choose sin over freedom it affects the dynamics of our relationship with God and others. When I say something hurtful to my husband it doesn't mean I'm not his wife anymore, but if I don't admit that I was wrong and ask for his forgiveness, it will affect our relationship.

The root of sin and the resolution of forgiveness have something to do with our pride.

You should never feel pressured to admit anything you've done to someone you don't trust, and some confessions are best handled in the safe confidentiality of a meeting with a pastor or someone who can hold the weight of your burden. When we pull our sins out of hiding and expose them to the light of God and others, they lose their power to harass, accuse, and lie to us about who we are or what people will think when they find us out.

The root of sin and the resolution of forgiveness have something to do with our pride. To forgive and receive forgiveness both require us to set aside our pride. Jesus lived a powerful life of humility, and growing in the humility of forgiving and being forgiven is part of becoming more like him.

REFLECTION: THE JESUS PRAYER

On Week 2, Day 2, we tried breath prayer. Today we will try a very specific breath prayer from the Eastern Christian tradition: the Jesus Prayer.

Lord Jesus Christ, Son of God, *(as we breathe in)*

have mercy on me, a sinner. *(as we breathe out)*

This prayer is based on the cries to Jesus made by ten lepers, a tax collector, and a blind man on different occasions in Luke's Gospel (Luke 17:13; 18:14, 38).

As a breath prayer, it's meant to be easy to recite throughout the day to stay in conversation with God (1 Thessalonians 5:16-18). As a repeated prayer, it habituates us in calling out to Jesus. The first time I prayed it, I felt awkward and maybe falsely humble, praying, "Have mercy on me, a sinner." Oof. I don't want to spoil this one, but this prayer certainly challenged my pride. There was something about borrowing words from the blind and lame who knew their need. It had been a while since I stepped out from behind my church smile, calling on God from my own posture of need. Asking for mercy is vulnerable, and receiving it is intimate.

Recite this prayer, using your breath, five times now. Notice how the prayer changes with tone and emphasis. Try making this breath prayer a part of your day today and tomorrow. May mercy find you.

DAY 4

PRAYER: FASTING

Fasting has served potent purposes throughout history; it was a means of prayer for Jesus, has been a church practice for centuries, and was even a practice of God's people in the Old Testament. It is a spiritual habit we should not ignore. As we end this study together, fasting could be a means to pray over the next twenty-four hours or seven days or thirty days.

Fasting is responsive. When major spiritual milestones occur in our life, especially challenging ones, one way to grieve and look to God for guidance through that valley of the shadow is fasting. In his book on fasting for the Ancient Practices series, Scot McKnight says that biblical "fasting is a response to a grievous sacred moment." For example, Ahab responds in repentance by fasting not to earn forgiveness but as a grieved response to the seriousness of what he has done. Jesus fasted in response to his commission to ministry, knowing his road to the cross would be difficult. Fasting not only manifested his dependence on God but also focused and strengthened him for the road ahead. Other sacred moments like death, urgent needs, or sickness may also elicit a response of fasting. When we let our bodies ache and hunger as our souls do, we may find ourselves satisfied by God in ways that food cannot.

Fasting is representative. Fasting is a spiritual discipline intended to unite our bodies with our souls. Our spiritual hunger is represented in our physical hunger like a metaphor that comes to life in all sensory dimensions. It is both a means of expressing our spiritual hunger through our bodies and receiving spiritual nurturing that satisfies our bodies.

Fasting is receiving, not earning. It is not about depriving ourselves or sacrificing pleasure to earn something from God. God does not owe us anything for trying harder, and we can't manipulate him to move on our behalf by our asceticism. It is undoubtedly not about earning something we already have. Fasting increases our awareness of God because it increases our dependence on him.

> "Fasting confirms our utter dependence upon God by finding in him a source of sustenance beyond food."
>
> **DALLAS WILLARD**

Food fast. Traditionally a food fast involves only drinking water or nutritious juice from sundown to sundown. It could also be as simple as skipping a single meal. Before you fast, please consult a doctor or nutritionist if you have any complicating health concerns, or if this is the first time you have ever fasted. If you feel severely tired, nauseous, or dizzy, you may need to eat something and try a simpler fast. If controlling your body's relationship with food has been difficult for you in the past, try a focus fast instead.

Focus fast. The Bible describes food fasting, but Christians have also used other forms of fasting throughout history. You may notice that connecting with God is difficult because you are too distracted or busy. In that case, you might try a fast from indulgences that interfere with your connection to God. For example, if you notice that it is hard for you to wake up in the morning to pray, you might try to eliminate things that get in the way of waking up sharp and rested. For example, TV, alcohol, staying out, or even reading late can affect our mental function. If you find that you are crashing in the afternoon you might try to eliminate sugar. If you are more tempted to marathon watch content late at night, consider abstaining from late nights by giving yourself an earlier bedtime. Think about times of your day when you most struggle to connect with God or honor him in your habits, and consider how abstaining from certain things might help you toward healthier goals. Design your own fast to make time and eliminate distractions to better connect with God.

How could fasting play a role in your life right now? What sort of fast might be the most helpful?

DAY 5

PRACTICE: PRAYER DAY

We live in a fast-paced, distracted, interrupted, and seemingly inescapable world—which is exactly why we must escape it occasionally. Retreats set aside the chaos of our everyday mental load so that we can think, feel, and work deeply. Retreats help our bodies and minds rest. So many of us long for, even pray for, wisdom, joy, peace, and energy for resilience but don't make space for God to answer us. As a result, we fail to create opportunities to breathe deeply or receive the gifts God has for us in our season. Now is the time to do that.

There are many reasons people don't think they can take a one-day retreat; by far, the most common are:

- I don't have time.

- I don't have money.

- I think I'll hate it.

- I don't know what to do.

I don't have time. Very few of us have excess time, but we all make time for what is important to us. Time is a stretchy thing; you can prioritize, work ahead, or delegate to free up some time. You might try to make a smaller escape for your first retreat, but try to block off and protect at least three hours of your time. Eventually, eighteen to twenty-four hours will feel perfect. It will be a sacrifice but a worthwhile one.

I don't have money. It is possible to find a retreat center through a Catholic church or even a public venue that will rent a spare but comfortable room at a very affordable rate. Still, it is also possible to have a prayer day free of cost. You might get creative about staying in someone else's home to sleep or sleeping in your bed but creating extensive boundaries around your time to make it distraction free, maybe even spending a good deal of time outside.

I think I'll hate it. You're an extrovert—or at least not a monk. You cannot imagine having hours alone in silence or solitude. Stepping away from the hustle or comfort of our worlds can be scary, so deep thinking and feeling and working are intimidating. We're not always sure we are ready to let the waters be still enough to reveal what is underneath. Rest is not something most of us are great at, but it is something we can learn. God designed rest as a vital rhythm to keep our souls from exhaustion and anxiety. Rest and retreat are investments in who you are and all you do. They are skills worth learning. Also, keep reading because a prayer day does not mean you are praying for eight hours straight.

I don't know what to do. You can plan your time in any number of ways. The most important thing about this time is that you make yourself available to God with your presence, attention, and conversation. Tell him what you think and need, and leave silence to listen for his response.

Everyone should plan to:

1. Disconnect from technology. Unplug from the internet. If possible, leave the number of the place you are staying and turn your cell phone off, or only allow calls on your phone from emergency contacts. Begin with silence and reflection.

2. Don't ignore your body. Your body and your soul are connected. Walk, stretch, hike, run, paddle, or do an activity that incorporates your body.

3. Receive rest as a gift from God. Enjoy sleep, silence, food, and the invitation to step away from your usual mental and physical load.

4. Spend time reading and meditating on your Bible and talking and listening to God. Give him your attention.

5. Surrender your plan at the beginning. You may have come to this time looking for an answer or an experience, but be open to receiving what God gives.

6. End the time with silence and reflection on where you noticed God's gifts or presence.

Depending on how you best connect with God (see the Week 4 Group Session for ideas), you may want to try any of these ideas that appeal to you:

1. Choose a book of the Bible to read and study.

2. Choose a Scripture to memorize.

3. Pay attention to nature.

4. Create music.

5. Create art.

6. Plan to fast.

7. Bring a good book that draws your mind to God and some light reading just for pleasure and to relax your mind.

8. Bring some soul stretching or soul sabbath exercises from this book that you would love to do or process further.

Think of how you can incorporate the Lord's Prayer or pieces of this study on your retreat. Are there activities you want to revisit? Study days you missed and want to catch up on? Intentions to revisit (Week 1, Day 5)? Bring your workbook along with you. Ask people from your group session how you can enable each other to take a prayer day (maybe you can swap caregiving responsibilities or pitch in to rent a cabin together). Enjoy your time away and find someone to process your experience with when you return. If you post pictures on social media, I would love to see them! Tag me! (@lizditty on Instagram, @lizditter on Twitter/X)

EPILOGUE

For thine is the kingdom, and the power,
and the glory, for ever and ever. Amen.

The function of Prayer is not to influence God,
but rather to change the nature
of the one who prays.

SØREN KIERKEGAARD

MANY PEOPLE SPEAK OF ELIJAH hearing God's voice outside a cave
on Mount Sinai. I had just finished writing a book about hearing God's voice
and had somehow failed to mention Elijah at all, but I started spending time
in his story as I was preparing content for subsequent retreats that I led around
the theme of hearing God's voice. The longer I spent in Elijah's story, the more
I became amazed by how he *spoke* to God, not just how he heard him. The idea
that James would claim that you and I are just as human as Elijah was, and could
pray those same prayers (James 5:17), seemed unbelievable until I recognized
that Elijah's prayers sounded a lot like the prayers Jesus said I should pray too.

Elijah's life has an incredible highlight reel, but the writer of his story did
not leave the hard parts out. It's just easy to skip over them. When I took my
time in the broken expectations and long years between big moments, the
loneliness and the burned-out zeal that brought Elijah's cave prayer *before*
God's well-known "whisper" were what resonated.

I made my own way to that holy mountain, nearly fainting in depression
and loneliness on the path. Praying for ravens . . . and then that same week
having a murder of crows alight from a tree as I walked by. Like Elijah re-
tracing the steps of Moses, I tried to follow the trail the prophet left. Some
scholars think that the apostle Paul took the same pilgrimage (Galatians 1:17),
and the Gospel writers seem to allude to this holy mountain in the picture

painted of Jesus taking James, John, and Peter up with him to pray on the Mount of Transfiguration—it seems all the zealots end up on God's mountains, and in the wilderness surrounding them.

I'd love to offer a final blessing for you as we turn the final pages of this book. I hope that following Elijah's steps has led you to Jesus as well, that Jesus' prayer and the different ways of praying that have led Jesus' people into conversation with God have formed an easy path to follow. I hope you were surprised a little by the fact that no one—not Moses or Elijah or Jesus himself—had an easy life, that the pain has never meant God didn't care, that his goodness breaks into the dark, and his faithfulness has never failed yet, that God is surprisingly easy and wonderful to talk to. I hope some of the conversations you've had with God and each other over the last six weeks have changed you, and that the world will never be the same.

BENEDICTION

Blessed are you, whose voice is still growing,

Who are learning the language of honest feelings, thoughts,
and desires.

Blessed are you, also, whose voice has grown tired,

Who wander in the wilderness,

Not knowing why you are alone,

Wondering if promises were broken and if they were yours or God's.

May the Holy Spirit translate your ache that is too hard
to pray in words,

As Jesus Christ lives to intercede for you,

To a heavenly Father who sees you, knows all that you need,
and cares for you deeply.

May you have courage in the desolate dryness of drought,

To cry out, "Hear me, God."

And look to the sky with an expectation that he is faithful.

Whether it is lightning, or a cloud the size of a pomegranate,
or simply silence that comes,

May you, blessed one, find rest in your belovedness,

Believing that somehow, even when,

Especially when,

Your body, or mind, or spirit are convinced they cannot continue,

You are seen, known, advocated for, and heard.

Faithful God, hear our prayers.

Because he turned his ear to me,
I will call on him as long as I live.
PSALM 116:2

FINAL REFLECTION

Flip back to your prayer day from Week 1. Remember those first prayers of intention that you prayed? Let's revisit those and reflect on the all the prayers we've prayed since.

How have your hopes changed or been met over the course of this study?

How have you engaged with your fears over the past weeks?

How has your posture shifted as you pray? (Week 1, Day 1)

How did you do with your weekly prayer goals?

As you look at every prayer time recorded on the chart (and any that were missed), I hope you feel God's delight in your intention to spend time with him and every imperfect human effort you made to prioritize that relationship.

How could you celebrate or commemorate all your prayers God has heard?

WEEKLY PRAYER GOAL	M	Tu

W	Th	F	Sa	Su

FIGURE CREDITS

ABOUT THE AUTHOR

Liz Ditty is a spiritual director, author, preacher, and teacher currently guiding transformative prayer retreats at Mount Hermon Conference Center, nestled in the coastal redwoods of California. A Silicon Valley native and Western Seminary graduate, Liz's central purpose in all she writes and teaches is to gently draw attention to God's presence in our actual—often challenging—lives. Alongside her supportive husband, two children, and spirited dog, Liz finds joy in sparking connection and community with all her people.

DISCOVER MORE AT
WWW.LIZDITTY.COM.

A NEW BIBLE STUDY EXPERIENCE FROM INTERVARSITY PRESS

These Bible studies offer you a fresh opportunity to engage with Scripture. Each study includes:

- weekly sessions for a group of any size
- access to weekly teaching videos
- five days of individual study and reflection each week

The refreshing, accessible, and insightful content from trusted Bible teachers will encourage you in your faith!

With guidance from trusted Bible teachers, this new collection of Bible studies invites groups and individuals to take a closer look at Scripture and offers practices that create space for prayer and worship, lament, and wonder. Each six to eight week study explores Scripture through a thematic lens, beginning each week with a group session that includes both video teaching and discussion questions, followed by five days of individual study and reflection.

Like this book?

Scan the code to discover more content like this!

Get on IVP's email list to receive special offers, exclusive book news, and thoughtful content from your favorite authors on topics you care about.

InterVarsity Press

IVPRESS.COM/BOOK-QR